Gentrification and Inequality in Brooklyn

Gentrification and Inequality in Brooklyn

The New Kids on the Block

Judith N. DeSena

LEXINGTON BOOKS

A division of
ROWMAN & LITTLEFIELD PUBLISHERS, INC.
Lanham • Boulder • New York • Toronto • Plymouth, UK

LEXINGTON BOOKS

A division of Rowman & Littlefield Publishers, Inc.
A wholly owned subsidiary of The Rowman & Littlefield Publishing Group, Inc.
4501 Forbes Boulevard, Suite 200
Lanham, MD 20706

Estover Road
Plymouth PL6 7PY
United Kingdom

British Library Cataloguing in Publication Information Available

Library of Congress Cataloging-in-Publication Data

DeSena, Judith N.
Gentrification and inequality in Brooklyn : the new kids on the block / Judith N. DeSena.
p. cm.
Includes bibliographical references and index.
ISBN-13: 978-0-7391-2342-3 (cloth : alk. paper)
ISBN-10: 0-7391-2342-4 (cloth : alk. paper)
eISBN: 978-0-7391-3809-0
1. Gentrification—New York (State)—Greenpoint (New York) 2. Urban renewal—New York (State)—Greenpoint (New York) 3. Greenpoint (New York, N.Y.)—Economic conditions. 4. Greenpoint (New York, N.Y.)—Social conditions. I. Title.
HT177.N5D47 2009
307.2'160974723—dc22

2009009959

Printed in the United States of America

∞™ The paper used in this publication meets the minimum requirements of American National Standard for Information Sciences—Permanence of Paper for Printed Library Materials, ANSI/NISO Z39.48-1992.

Contents

Acknowledgments

I would like to take this opportunity to acknowledge those who assisted me through this major undertaking. My husband, Neil Sheehan, tirelessly read every word I wrote, good and bad, and also engaged in endless discussions about this analysis. For him in my life and in my work I am forever grateful. My children, Francis and Paul, who keep me energized to do this work, opened many doors for me in the community. Through their lives I gained knowledge. I thoroughly enjoy growing together. Through many years in the same department, my dear friend and colleague, William DiFazio, offered me insight into this book when our conversations were about a completely different matter. I thank him for his intellect, his time, and his friendship. Many graduate students had a hand in some aspect of this book, and I am grateful for their assistance and good humor through the process: Daniel Douglas, Maureen Elliot, Alexis Figueroa, Lamia Vucetovic, and Kendra Chiu. I would also like to thank the support of St. John's University, particularly Dawn Esposito, Jeffrey Fagen, and Julia Upton, for providing a research leave and reduced teaching in some years while I worked on this book. I also appreciate the comments of the anonymous reviewer for Lexington Books. I am confident that they have contributed to a broader analysis of gentrification. Finally, I would like to thank the residents of Greenpoint, old and new, for allowing me into their separate communities.

Introduction

This book is about the process of gentrification in a Brooklyn neighborhood in New York. It focuses on the arrangement of groups, of gentry and working class residents within the community. Gentrification represents another cycle of neighborhood change. The neighborhood of Greenpoint, the focus of this study, has for most of its existence been a working class community inhabited by immigrants and later generations of those immigrants' families. It is now experiencing an influx of more formally educated and affluent residents relative to the long-term, sometimes lifelong, population. This book ultimately highlights the central theme of social class distinctions in a changing community.

With a multitude of ethnic groups, several religions, and now a mixture of social classes, on an everyday basis, Greenpoint is generally an orderly place within one of America's oldest and largest cities. On most days, nothing too extraordinary happens. People carry out their daily lives racing to and from work, moving children around, frequenting local retail establishments and recreational facilities. Even within the context of difference, both cultural and social class, people appear to get along. There is rarely physical violence between groups. In a community such as Greenpoint people engage in "parallel play," interacting next to each other while focused on their own group and activities. In his study of Boston (1999), Daniel Monti states,

> It is not immediately apparent how all these different persons residing in the same place figure out that they can work together or at least do not have to fight all the time . . . Kindergarten teachers call it "parallel play" . . . Parallel play operates in a similar way in cities where different and sometimes quarrelsome groups must stumble into a state of mutual regard . . . When one set of them puts together groups of their own or watches how other persons do it, this is how

> they learn about each other. It is also how they come to see the possibility and necessity of working together at least part of the time . . . Cities are really big parallel playpens" (Monti 1999, p. 206).

Supporting Monti's contention about parallel play is a remark made by a Greenpoint resident and mother as she observed people gathering while waiting for children to be dismissed from school. She said,

> You see it in the schoolyard as we pick the kids up. There's groups. There's us, the old neighborhood, the YUPPIES, the immigrants. The YUPPIES say, 'we're integrating.' They're not integrating! They don't want to integrate. They want to be their own group.

The groups she described are engaged in parallel play.

In Greenpoint for example, McCarren Park is a large complex of three parks serving the communities of Greenpoint and Williamsburg and marks a boundary between these neighborhoods. On weekends and holidays, the parks are crowded with residents of all ages speaking numerous languages engaged in various activities. Particularly in the summer, some families' barbecue, couples picnic drinking wine from festive glasses, and immigrant youths play soccer and cricket. They operate individually in unison. In addition, in another park in the community during the summer months, a variety of films have been shown on Friday nights. There too is a mixing of groups of gentry, working class, and immigrant residents who gather to cool off accompanied by some entertainment. On one such occasion, a working class man commented, "I watched my neighbors come here with trays of hors d'oeuvres!"

Neighborhoods like Greenpoint are the places in cities in which tensions and disagreements are negotiated and people learn to work things out to some conclusion. In neighborhoods residents cannot avoid each other. They can either escape for a time, move, or engage in some level of dialogue. This is also a way that neighbors who are different from each other learn about each other, learn from each other, and become somewhat like each other, while at the same time possibly remaining unequal. New York City's folklore claims to have a resident from every country around the world. Historically and presently, it is in New York City's many diverse neighborhoods that people from different cultures with different languages and religions learn about each other's ways of life and also become acculturated, integrating habits of another group into their own lives. For example, in Greenpoint, a resident explained to me that as a young man he was often asked by a rabbi to turn on the lights of a synagogue located on his street during Jewish holidays. After obliging, the rabbi would offer him a "shot" of liquor in gratitude. The man was Catholic and through his assistance he learned a bit more about Jewish religious customs. And historically, White Anglo-Saxon Protestant groups learned about peasant immigrants from their migration to neighborhoods of New York City. In this way we are all social observers, studying one another, taking from each other, and integrating new ways as our ways.

It has been argued that an American culture and American cities developed in this way based on these multicultural interactions. In sociology, the urban culturalist perspective presents this view (Borer 2006). According to this perspective, there is a relationship between culture and places in which shared meanings get constructed, negotiated, and reworked. For urban culturalists, neighborhoods are places in which ways of life are constantly negotiated and continually changing.

> Culture is never a matter of pure consensus . . . What matters are the shared meanings that can create connections between individuals, groups, and something larger and more lasting than both" (Borer 2006, p. 192).

American culture and life in cities are created in this way. Culture is created in everyday life. Greenpoint's local cultures can be analyzed using this framework.

MAKING ACCOMMODATIONS

Residents of Greenpoint, with all their differences, arrive at a level of accommodation in which they are able to live together in a neighborhood. In many ways, the mere density and attendant physical proximity of residents in a neighborhood in New York City forces a dialogue among people regardless of their dissimilar social characteristics. Since they cannot completely avoid each other, perhaps people become more alike than they will ever be equal. There is a process of homogenization that seems to occur.

In everyday life in Greenpoint, there are instances in which "bridges" are built, connecting individuals from different social classes. It is not uncommon for gentry and working class renters and homeowners to bid each other "good morning" or to gesture "hello" with a nod or a wave of the hand. Working class and gentry neighbors will stop and chat to each other about vacations. Recently, I listened to such a conversation in which two residents respectively discussed Milan, Italy. Homeowners will also collaborate on solving a problem that their individual houses exhibit. For example, as New York City faces somewhat changing weather patterns and encounters torrential rains that on one occasion a few summers ago paralyzed the subway system from flooding, many homes in Greenpoint were met with sewer backflow into their basements. Gentry, working class, and immigrant homeowners would stop each other on the street and talk about what they may have learned from other sources in hope of resolving the problem. They shared information and also shared individual decisions made for each home.

As working class and immigrant homeowners living in the neighborhood's historic district confront the need for a permit from the Landmarks Preservation Commission in order to renovate their buildings' facades, such as replacing windows or exterior doors and shingles, they will often employ the services of local, gentry architects to navigate through the process. Gentry residents, including tenants, have introduced the "stoop sale" to the neighborhood. This is a city version of the suburban garage sale in which a household's used items are displayed on the street, in front of their residence, and are for sale. On any day posters are hung from street poles announcing the date, time, and place of an upcoming stoop sale. Working class residents can be seen mimicking this practice and holding stoop sales, an example of becoming alike. Gentry residents have also brought with them the practice of bicycling to Greenpoint on a much larger scale than had existed prior to their residence. New York City's government supports this habit as part of its "green" campaign and has drawn bike lanes on local streets and provided bike racks outside parks and the entrance to some subway stations. Working class and immigrant inhabitants are riding bicycles more often and can also be found participating in the global biking phenomenon.

Greenpoint's long-term, working class and immigrant, resident homeowners accommodate gentry newcomers because of the higher rents they bring to them. Thus, long-term residents have adapted to a gentry renter's trumpet playing out his apartment window, or another gentry renter spending the day sitting on a front stoop sketching nearby buildings and photographing local scenes, or another having a party in which guests arrive by bicycle and lock them to poles, trees, and gates nearby the host's apartment.

Much accommodation takes place around children, especially between mothers with a focus on children. In the spring, mothers of young children will see each other on the street and exchange information and opinions about schools they have toured for their child's kindergarten enrollment. One morning a woman who was rushing past me, "I'm going to another tour. PS 110."

Both gentry and working class mothers whose children have started preschool or to a lesser extent, kindergarten will stop and ask each other how their child is doing making the transition during the first few weeks of school. Observers will hear,

> She cried for an hour! My heart was broken. I called later that morning and [the teacher] told me she was fine. She stopped crying after I left.

On other occasions, gentry and working class mothers will chat about which extracurricular activities their child will enroll. "Is she taking ballet? Class starts Saturday." Which was answered, "I think we'll be doing soccer." And for older children, gentry and working class mothers will discuss the high school application process, their opinions about schools they have visited, and ultimately, their child's final admission and placement.

Gentry and working class mothers and their children also interact at children's birthday parties. Children's closest friends from school are often invited to a celebration, or at times, an entire school class is invited. Just recently, a boy's second grade class was invited by his gentry parents to an amusement park to celebrate his birthday. In the past, preschool classes were invited to a local restaurant owned by the parents of children enrolled. It is during these occasions that mothers in particular share and disseminate information. In these instances, mothering appears to transcend social class.

ANOTHER APPROACH

The reader should know that the author, having just chosen to initially describe and discuss the urban cultural approach in sociology, takes a different approach. The book that follows, as previously mentioned in the first paragraph of this introduction, presents a serious challenge to the limitations of the urban cultural framework and suggests that class, not culture, is the more critical variable in the lives of ordinary people.

A cultural approach to the study of gentrification lacks depth and the very essence of a sociological analysis. It examines everyday interactions of civility in which residents of cities engage for social order and functionality. Borer includes Gans's book *The Urban Villagers* (1962) as part of the urban culturalist genre. Gans disagrees with Borer's categorization and explains that during his study of the West End, the city of Boston had bigger plans that West Enders did not fit into (Gans 2007). Gans explains that West Enders lacked political power to be of any concern to the city of Boston, since the city needed the urban renewal funds for its coffers flowing from the federal government. In fact, Gans goes on to say,

> culture per se is not a useful explanatory tool because it is generally devoid of agency and can quickly turn into an Uncaused Cause. As a descriptive tool, culture runs the danger of restating already well-known observations in technical language, thus giving ammunition to those claiming sociology to be unnecessary (Gans 2007, pp. 159–60).

Just because people are not engaged in physical fighting in the street, and exhibit accommodation to each other does not mean that they come to be alike more than they will ever be equal. Being unequal makes us different, even if we *appear* to act the same and to get along. That is precisely the point of the life's work of many sociologists. Being unequal creates power relations and power dynamics that involve tensions and disagreements over resources and amenities. In fact, Marx and Engels contend, "Political power, properly so called, is merely the organized power of one class for oppressing another" (2002, p. 244).

"[And] culturalism cannot explain power" (Gans 2007, p. 159). Borer himself admits,

> And even though communities are collective accomplishments, not everyone plays an equal role in making these decisions or practices them exactly the same way (Borer 2006, p. 186).

Thus, power, inequality, and difference are implicit in community building.

In a discussion about ethnic groups in *The American City: A Social and Cultural History* (1999), Monti writes,

> Success came with a price. There have been many occasions when representatives of more established groups tried to encourage newcomers to think and act more like the old-timers or actively punished the newcomers for being different. To a great extent the newcomers actually did become a whole lot more like the persons who already were here. However, they also managed to retain some important ideas and practices that were connected to their native cultures or early experiences in a new land (p. 379).

The newcomers in Greenpoint are not becoming like the people already there. The remaining chapters of this book will specify various actions of the gentry and working class exhibited side by side, sometimes in conflict because of social class differences. Their parallel play, in the final analysis, is about dominance and eventual takeover of the neighborhood by the gentry class. This change evolves over time, but ultimately, the working class and immigrants lose out.

This book focuses on gentrification in Greenpoint, Brooklyn. It is an analysis of neighborhood change with a focus on social class. It highlights how social class differences lead to the creation and maintenance of parallel cultures within the neighborhood. Unlike the relationship described by Monti between old-timers and newcomers, gentrifiers in Greenpoint, who are the newcomers, are not assimilating in the same way. Gentrifiers spend time among their own. According to Monti and Borer this is how people learn from each other. However, "parallel play" in Greenpoint is segregation by social class between the gentry and the working class, which serves to perpetuate social inequality.

The following chapters look to examine the process of gentrification by uncovering the underlying tensions and power dynamics that exist in this neighborhood as gentrifiers develop into the dominant group of a previously stable, working class community, and Greenpoint moves toward a complete transition by social class. In the chapters that follow I seek to illustrate this theme by exploring the everyday struggles between gentry and working class residents and the choices made to separate rather than integrate by social class regarding children's recreational activities, schooling, and the process of rezoning Greenpoint's waterfront for residential use.

The subsequent portrait uses the brush of sociology to highlight social class rather than culture. I hope my work manages to ignite a spark that can contribute to a dialogue about social class and its part in a changing working class community.

Chapter One

Gentrification, Segregation, and Negotiation in the City

This book is an analysis of social class and the ways that it is manifested and unfolds in an urban neighborhood. It is a qualitative study of gentrification in Greenpoint, Brooklyn, a community in New York City. The investigation goes beyond studying housing, displacement, and explicit class conflict and class struggle, the focus of most research, and analyzes the process of gentrification in what had traditionally been a working class and low-income community. Furthermore, unlike earlier research, which characterizes gentrifiers primarily as singles and young, childless couples, this research examines gentrifying families. This study is accomplished by focusing on the different positions taken by gentrifiers and long-term residents regarding each group's connection to and participation in the local community. Under examination are the ways in which the process of gentrification affects ordinary people (working class and low-income) and gentrifiers (middle class and upper–middle class residents). This study contributes to urban theory by analyzing what happens "in between" the causes and consequences of gentrification. The book arrives at theory, which argues that in the course of their everyday lives, gentrifiers create segregation by social class, which perpetuates the current system of social stratification and ultimately reproduces social inequality. Thus, gentrification creates greater social inequality.

Put simply, this is a study of neighborhood change in the form of gentrification. However, the developmental stages of gentrification in Greenpoint have varied from those outlined by Burgess and the Chicago School. For Burgess, neighborhood change involved a process of invasion and succession of groups of socially and culturally diverse people. One stage he discusses is "reaction," in which an existing population responds to newcomers. This can range from mild comments or letter writing to violence and property damage. Burgess's model is based primarily on ethnic and racial transition in neighborhoods.

Greenpoint has been a working class community since its development, with factories lining the waterfront and manufacturing interspersed among homes. Many locals were employed at these factories, some of which were union shops. During the 1950s, Greenpoint experienced immigration from Puerto Rico. In the 1960s and 1970s as city neighborhoods experienced white flight because of suburbanization and an increase of minority residents, Greenpoint maintained itself as a primarily white community with a relatively smaller proportion of Latino/as (DeSena 1990; 2005). The 1980s brought another wave of Polish immigrants as martial law was instituted in Poland in response to the Solidarity movement. Gentrification represents the latest transition for this community. The neighborhood never experienced racial transition, but segregated ethnic diversity. It is presently experiencing a transition of social class. Yet, unlike the community's response to the in-migration of Latino/as, which took the form of various informal strategies to defend against their residence (see DeSena 2005 for a discussion of these strategies), Greenpoint residents did not "react" to gentrification.

This book also highlights community activism. Greenpoint has a high degree of social capital and a long history of social activism and community organization (DeSena 1998). Long-term residents are well versed at attending meetings, "turning out" for rallies, and marching on City Hall. The community is engaged in ongoing negotiation with the City of New York regarding municipal services and community development. During the period of data collection, the community was the focus of one of the largest land use rezoning projects in the history of New York City. This is because the political economy regards the Brooklyn waterfront as the latest terrain of capital investment. Hence, this book also investigates local activism directed toward decision making affecting the community and negotiation with the political economy within the context of gentrification.

DOING THE STUDY

This is a qualitative study of gentrification in Greenpoint, which means that I have spent years engaged in various community settings with both gentrifiers and ordinary residents. This investigation was carried out through participant observation, interviews, and content analysis. I have been studying Greenpoint for close to thirty years; this is my third book analyzing the community. Gentrification has been my focus since 1996 as I moved around playgrounds and playgroups within the neighborhood with my children and met many (mostly) mothers and children who were relatively new residents and did not have the social ties or attachments of long-term residents. Their professional and technical status quickly became obvious to me as we discussed work, experiences in college and graduate school, residential history, and aspirations for our children's education. My research style was unobtrusive in that I listened closely to the daily conversations among mothers and asked questions of them as a neighbor and "new" mother. In some instances, formal interviews were conducted. Since then, I have been spending time with both lifelong working class residents and relatively newer, upper middle class residents. This enables me to hear about their concerns and opinions about life and the world. I am able to accomplish this by moving in and out of assorted local settings that also allowed opportunities for comparison.

FRAMING THIS STUDY

The concept of gentrification is being defined as "the conversion of socially marginal and working class areas of the central city to middle-class [and elite] residential use" (Zukin 1987, p. 129). Although the literature refers to gentrifiers as middle class, this book considers them upper middle class with more money and job security than the traditional middle class. Research on gentrification focuses primarily on the causes and consequences of this urban process. Analyses fall into two major theoretical perspectives, ecological theory and critical theory (Wittberg 1992). The ecologists examine the needs, tastes, and desires of populations, which are responsible for precipitating neighborhood change in the form of gentrification (Laska and Spain 1980; Friedenfels 1992). Research from an ecological perspective argues that gentrification has numerous causes. For example, Berry (1973) contends that gentrification stems from there being a greater need for housing by baby boomers, low vacancy rates, and the relatively high cost of suburban housing. Cybriwsky (1978) views competition among social classes for urban space as a cause of gentrification. Laska and Spain (1980) point to the cost of new housing and commuting as a cause for people remaining in the city. Long (1980) views lower fertility rates and smaller household size as factors precipitating gentrification since less living space is needed relative to larger families. Additional demographic factors that focus on a changing family are also cited as contributors to gentrification. These include: nontraditional living arrangements, an increase of age at first marriage, later birth of first child, an increasing rate of single and married women entering into the paid labor force, and an increase of dual-wage-earner families. These changing demographics would account for lower fertility rates and smaller household size. Also included in this perspective are studies that examine the strategies used to create and produce gentrification and preserve upper middle class status in specific neighborhoods. Kasinitz's study of Boerum

Hill in Brooklyn (1998) indicates various strategies used by some residents to manufacture gentrification while at the same time, their intention is to prevent deterioration. According to Kasinitz, these strategies include constructing a local history that could be advertised, renaming the neighborhood or portions of it, producing house tours to "show off" the neighborhood, and participating in historic preservation by the creation of a historic district. Krase's study of Lefferts Manor in Brooklyn (1982) discusses the use of a restrictive covenant in maintaining housing as "single family only" in order to keep the community middle class.

Critical theorists, on the other hand, view the causes of gentrification as stemming from actions of the political economy; namely, the investments of capital and the policies of the state (Abu-Lughod 1994; Smith 1996; Zukin 1982; 1987; Fitch 1993). Zukin's study of SoHo in New York City (1982) indicates that the political economy takes on a "cultural" strategy that supports art and historic preservation. In the case of SoHo, the ultimate result is not only gentrification but also the eventual attraction of an elite community. Smith's research on class struggle over Tompkins Square Park in New York City (1996), examines clashes between the political economy and ordinary people. In one conflict, city government imposed a curfew on the park. Ordinary people attempted to "retake the city" by rioting against the police and engaging in other protest activities. According to Smith, some residents believed that the city's claim to "clean up" the park of homeless individuals and drug traffic was actually a move to facilitate even more gentrification on Manhattan's Lower East Side. Like Zukin, Smith believes that the culture industry adds to the growth of gentrification. Smith (1996) views the notion of "back to the city," a phrase associated with gentrification, as meaning that capital investment, not people, moved back to the city. For him, gentrification represents postmodern urbanism.

Some scholars discuss a change in the process of gentrification in the 1990s. Smith (1996) contends that due to the 1987 stock market crash and ensuing recession, degentrification has occurred. According to Smith, there was "a much reduced rate and impact of gentrification in favor of a more unevenly developed, polarized, and segregated city . . . the revanchist city is becoming a powerful reality" (p. 94). For Smith, upper middle class and elite gentrifiers found themselves with lowered property values and forced interactions with minority groups, immigrants, and women as they competed for the urban terrain. Hackworth's study of three gentrifying neighborhoods in New York City (2002) argues that there have been changes in the process of gentrification since the recession of the 1990s. One major change is that the state is investing in the process more directly than in the past. Another change is that corporate developers are the initial migrants prior to gentrifiers, more so than before when they followed pioneers. In addition, actions by ordinary people against gentrification have been marginalized in that their concerns are dismissed by those in power.

The discourse on gentrification documents the benefits and costs of this process on the local community. The literature profiles most gentrifiers as affluent, young, single, urban professionals, and young, married couples who are both wage earners and have no children, or small families. This segment of the population is credited with revitalizing older, city neighborhoods, and by extension, the city itself through housing improvements and loft conversions, service upgrades, and an expansion of the local economy with the introduction of new restaurants and retail establishments. Lance Freeman's study of Harlem in Manhattan and Clinton Hill in Brooklyn (2006) indicates this point. He discusses the in-migration of whites to these predominantly black communities and examines what black residents think about this gentrification. He finds that on some level it is welcomed in these neighborhoods. Residents convey that with gentrification come better services and more amenities. Studies dealing with the consequences of gentrification on neighborhoods examine primarily housing and present increasing housing costs and displacement of existing populations as outcomes (Cybriwsky 1978; Marcuse 1986; LeGates and Hartman 1986). Thus, in general, the major consequence of gentrification documented in the literature is the displacement or "replacement" (Freeman and Braconi 2004) of ordinary people and small businesses to more affluent groups and sometimes elites, as well as the transition of "mom and pop" businesses to retail chains and boutiques. Another outcome is that ordinary people have fewer choices regarding places of residence, since affordable neighborhoods are diminished by gentrification. In her study of a community on Chicago's South Side, Boyd (2008) discusses "defensive development," which is an attempt to avoid the displacement of blacks by gentrifying whites. It involves "neighborhood-based strategies that are designed to build the economic strength of neighborhoods as a way of avoiding political and physical displacement by whites" (p. 756). Through this process, gentrification by blacks was facilitated. The community remained comprised of blacks, but its social class changed to include elites.

The dynamics of gentrification in a neighborhood and the way it affects community life, and the everyday lives of residents beyond housing, is an underrepresented area of scholarship. This study of Greenpoint attempts to address the void by examining the *process* of gentrification, the period of time prior to complete neighborhood change, and investigates the interactions of ordinary people and gentrifiers in a neighborhood for which they compete.

Feminist theory (Alonso 1980; Markusen 1981) also informs the discourse on gentrification. This approach views gentrification within the context of demographics portraying changes in women's lives. For example, as more women move into paid work, there is also a decrease in fertility rates and household size. Alonso (1980) argues that working women prefer living near their place of employment. With greater economic power, women have greater influence on the location of their family's residence. Like Alonso, Bondi (1994) views gentrification "as one of several spatial expressions of the changing character of work in women's lives" (p. 196). Thus, gentrification results from a shift in the position of women's lives. Moreover, for Markusen (1981) gentrification is an outcome of the feminist movement. She views gentrification as an opportunity to change patriarchal living arrangements as women acquire greater decision making.

The feminist literature examines gentrification in terms of women's relation to work, but it does not investigate women's activist behavior within the context of gentrification. In other words, there is a void in urban theory of studies analyzing the actions of women in shaping gentrification. Smith's study of gentrification on the Lower East Side of Manhattan (1996) calls for research examining women's roles in gentrification. Subsequent chapters of this book indicate ways that gentrification is shaped by women. A major way is by segregating the children of gentrifiers from their lower class peers and by socializing them to be members of a relatively entitled, privileged class. Thus, "women's work" in the process of gentrification is examined in this study. Consequently, feminism informs this book.

Unlike earlier research indicating that gentrifiers are primarily young singles or couples without children, Caulfield's study of Toronto (1994) argues that "gentrification is a housing form found quite suitable for child rearing by some contemporary middle class urbanites" (p. 77). In this study parents indicated their preference for downtown housing, close proximity to jobs and services used by the family, and ethnic, racial, and social class diversity. Research on gentrifying households with children is also an underrepresented area of inquiry. In general, the literature reveals that the quality of neighborhood schools is a major reason that couples with children decide against living in the city. LeGates and Hartman (1986) argue that "because inner city school systems are seldom good, few young parents will choose to settle in inner city neighborhoods if they have another choice" (p. 181). Thus, gentrifying families tend to prefer private schools in the city, or move to the suburbs to obtain what they perceive as a quality education for their children. Unlike this earlier research, chapter 5 examines the use of public schools by gentrifiers in Greenpoint, but instead of utilizing neighborhood public schools, they select those outside of the community. Moreover, the chapter also documents the activism of women gentrifiers regarding their children's schooling. Robson and Butler's study of London (2001) contends,

> The significance and role of education in gentrification processes cannot be generalized. What is crucial is the examination of cases, in particular the interaction between local educational infrastructures and the varying middle-class strategies designed to exploit them (p. 72).

Chapter 5 examines such a case.

GENTRIFICATION IN GREENPOINT

The following chapters will offer a social history and demographic description of Greenpoint, as well as factors precipitating gentrification. Greenpoint is presently a community with three major populations: long-term working class residents, Polish immigrants, and gentrifiers. The earlier gentrification of Williamsburg, a neighboring community, has had a spill-over effect into Greenpoint. Gentrifiers have been exploring Greenpoint for more living space at more affordable prices than in Williamsburg. In Greenpoint one can now observe factory loft conversions to residences and art galleries and sidewalk eateries on what were once desolate, industrial streets. For the most part, gentrifiers in Williamsburg are younger and more transient than those in Greenpoint.

Greenpoint has been a community envied. It was historically white, stable, affordable, physically well kept, with high occupancy rates, low crime, high levels of social capital, and a high degree of neighboring. Ironically, these very characteristics attracted gentrifiers. Its low-scale, small-town charm and relative affordability were appealing to gentrifiers as a place of residence. At the same time, as subsequent chapters will indicate, gentrifiers in Greenpoint do not participate in the predominate life of the community. They do not involve themselves in the very aspects of the community that attracted them to it in the first place. Instead, they segregate themselves from other white, working class and immigrant residents, and socialize and create community with other residents like themselves. As described by one resident gentrifier, "We liked that it was a neighborhood with other creative people like ourselves."

Furthermore, gentrifiers in Greenpoint convey a manner of entitlement to the neighborhood and impose their lifestyle and public practices on long-term residents instead of adapting to local ways. These differences of lifestyle and conflicting social norms will be discussed in the following chapters. In general, what has developed is a clash of lifestyles and social norms between ordinary, working class and immigrant residents and upper middle class gentrifiers. Gentrifiers, once attracted to the physical neatness of the housing stock, are now critical of its aluminum siding and instead support restoration to a building's original (historical) façade. Thus among other things, people's sense of aesthetics clash. Subsequently, a parallel culture for each group develops and ensues. The working class (and immigrants) continue to engage in traditional, local institutions (church, ethnic organizations, PTA), while gentrifiers create new social milieus (bars with sidewalk seating, art galleries, new community organizations).

The expected social and political liberalism of gentrifiers, which includes a philosophy of more economic, racial, and social equality and opportunities for all, is, in the final analysis, about self-interest disguised by political progressiveness. Once gentrifiers come to dominate a neighborhood, the community is replaced with dominant social norms and relations that are suitable and affordable for the gentry class and others like them. Ironically, the working class has traditionally been accused of racism. This study reveals that the gentry engage in classism, which can also translate into racism. The ultimate consequence of gentrification is the maintenance of the status quo in the form of the current system of social stratification and inequality.

Gentrification is an urban process occurring globally in various stages of development. City residents, urban planners, and local government policy makers often look to gentrification as a positive process that alleviates social problems. In other words, gentrification "sweeps away" deterioration and poverty and revitalizes the city (according to these policy makers), one neighborhood at a time. This is the current urban policy, which works hand in hand with global capitalism. The problem with this orientation is that the gentrification of working class communities literally destroys economic and social stability. This is done by creating speculation and displacement in neighborhoods where previously stable, well-maintained residential housing stock was already occupied, not vacant and blighted. Greenpoint did not need to be converted, saved, stabilized, revitalized, or "turned around." It was doing fine as a working class/immigrant neighborhood in an "outer borough" within New York City. The outer boroughs are presently the latest terrain of global capitalism. As individuals, the gentry bid higher for housing than the working class or immigrant groups. Each group forms a network within the community and operates to acquire resources for the group. The gentry will ultimately reign in Greenpoint because of their greater economic power. Therefore, this book indicates how on a community level, gentrification is helped along by the everyday actions of gentrifiers.

Chapter 2 discusses Greenpoint's social history and describes its physical space and social capital. Chapter 3 examines the population of Greenpoint in terms of social characteristics and discusses how neighborhood change in the form of gentrification came about. Chapter 4, "Gentrification in Everyday Life," investigates interactions on the street between ordinary residents and gentrifiers. It serves as a backdrop and offers a context for subsequent chapters. Chapter 5, "Gentrification and Local Schools: Women Shape the Urban Landscape," further develops theoretical ideas set forth in this chapter by focusing on the local elementary schools and investigating attendance by social class. Chapter 6, "Soccer Moms in the City," analyzes the perspective of parents toward the community by examining the ways in which they direct their children's play. This is accomplished through the lens of children's recreation. Chapters 5 and 6 in particular examine how women contribute to gentrification. Chapter 7, "Views of Manhattan for Sale: Rezoning for Residential Development on the East River," presents the issue of rezoning and planning Greenpoint's waterfront (the East River overlooking Manhattan) for residential use and examines the various players and their positions as the community decides the future of Greenpoint. "Class conflict," in the form of self interest, becomes evident with this issue. Conclusions are drawn in chapter 8, focusing on what these findings mean for the future of the city while also raising questions regarding the capacity by the working class to maintain a place in the city.

Chapter Two

The Neighborhood of Greenpoint

In its early history, Greenpoint was referred to as the "garden spot" of the world because of its green pastures and isolation. By the 1980s, it was described as "a tightly-knit ethnic community [where] . . . a feeling of small town friendliness and informality characterizes interchanges among residents" (New York City Landmarks Preservation Commission). More recently, this small-town appeal has attracted gentrification. This chapter discusses Greenpoint's location, physical development and built environment, social history, social activism, and community organization. This presentation lays the groundwork for a later discussion on gentrification.

THE PLACE

Greenpoint is a neighborhood at the northernmost tip of Brooklyn. In fact, it is a peninsula that is bound on the north and the east by the Newtown Creek and on the west by the East River. McCarren Park, a complex of three parks arranged for various recreational activities, is used as Greenpoint's southern boundary (although in the demographic description that follows, this geographic boundary and census tracts are not coterminous).

Greenpoint lies across the river from Manhattan. The Citicorp building on Manhattan's east side is visible from the tip of Greenpoint's major commercial center, looming far above the low-scale buildings in the community. Manhattan is easily accessible from Greenpoint by car. One can choose among the Williamsburg Bridge, the Queensborough Bridge (59th Street), or the Queens Midtown Tunnel. Without traffic congestion, it takes about fifteen minutes driving time with any of these crossings to get from Greenpoint to Manhattan. Greenpoint is also connected to neighborhoods in Queens (Long

Island City, Sunnyside, and Maspeth) by the Pulaski, the Greenpoint Avenue, and the Kosciusko bridges. The Kosciusko Bridge also links the Brooklyn-Queens Expressway with the Long Island Expressway.

Like much of New York City, Greenpoint is also served by public transportation. One mode of transportation is the Independent Subway Line—more specifically, the G train. The subway journey to Manhattan from Greenpoint is indirect: one must ride to Queens stations, Court Square or Queens Plaza, in order to board a Manhattan-bound train. The G train also runs through parts of Brooklyn and Queens; more specifically, from an area commonly referred to as "downtown Brooklyn" to Long Island City in Queens. Residents who live near the "northside" of Williamsburg (streets named North 1 through North 13) have access to the BMT Canarsie Line, the L train. It is a short ride (three stops) to the 14th Street and Union Square station in Manhattan where one can transfer to other trains. Public bus lines in Greenpoint follow nearly the same Brooklyn-Queens route as the Independent subway. None of the buses serving Greenpoint are Manhattan bound.

Adjacent to Greenpoint in Brooklyn, lying just across its southern boundary, is Williamsburg. Greenpoint and Williamsburg share the administration of many municipal services, and together, they make up Brooklyn's Community Board 1, an extension of New York City government in the community.

THE NEIGHBORHOOD'S BEGINNINGS

Greenpoint was purchased from the Canarsie Indians by the Dutch West India Company in 1638. A parcel of land, which included Bushwick, Williamsburg, and Greenpoint, was secured from the Indians for the price of "eight fathoms of duffels, eight strings of wampum, twelve kettles, eight chip axes, eight hatchets and some knives, beads, and awls" (Brooklyn Union Gas Company, 1). At that time, Greenpoint was part of the Township of Bushwick, which was governed by Peter Stuyvesant.

Greenpoint remained an isolated area for many years because it was surrounded by water on three sides and partially on the south by the Bushwick Creek. This creek was later filled and is presently McCarren Park. During the Revolutionary War, there were only five families in Greenpoint: the Bennets, Calyers, Meseroles, Provoosts, and Van Zandts. These families farmed the land with their slaves and transported their produce by boat across the East River to Manhattan. Some of the streets in Greenpoint presently carry the names of these families, a reminder of the neighborhood's history.

Greenpoint resisted commercial development until the late 1830s. In 1838 the first public highway, Franklin Turnpike, was completed. This highway included a bridge over Bushwick and Newtown creeks. It was Greenpoint's first link to the industrializing areas of Williamsburg and Astoria, Queens. The opening of this highway marked the end of Greenpoint's isolation and pastoral existence.

Like its neighboring communities, Greenpoint began to industrialize. A shipbuilding industry developed on the waterfront, employing over half of the local population, and was the major industry in Greenpoint until about 1870. A variety of vessels were built (clipper ships, steamships) by renowned shipbuilders, such as John Englis, Henry Steers, and John Ericcson. Ericcson was responsible for designing and building the *Monitor*, an ironclad ship, which is credited with changing the course of naval history. It saved the Union navy by defeating the Confederate *Merrimac* in the Civil War. The *Monitor* was built at the Continental Shipbuilding Corporation, which was located on Calyer Street in Greenpoint.

The growing shipbuilding industry attracted laborers from Ireland and later from Italy. Emigration from Ireland began around 1850 because of famine. By 1855, one third of New York City's voters were Irish (Glazer and Moynihan 1970). In the same year, Italians began crossing the Atlantic. However, it was not until the 1870s that mass migration from Italy began. Immigrants from both groups had few skills and little industrial training. The initial place of settlement in Greenpoint for both groups of immigrants was in its northern section, since that was the area that was first developed because of its proximity to waterfront industries.

Residential and shopping areas were developed in order to accommodate workers. Three- and four-story frame houses were built near the waterfront. The Astral Apartments, a six-story apartment complex, was built by Charles Pratt to lodge workers. In addition, brownstones were built along a few streets to house the local elite. By the mid 1840s, Protestant denominations opened churches. Greenpoint's first school also opened at this time. The first Catholic church was established in 1856.

Around 1850, a steam ferry service began, which ran from East 10th Street in Manhattan to Greenpoint Avenue. A second ferry was later established, which ran from East 23rd Street to Greenpoint Avenue. The ferry service was started by Neziah Bliss. Originally from Connecticut, Bliss married Mary Meserole, the daughter of one of Greenpoint's first families, and they made Greenpoint their home. Ferry service had a major influence on Greenpoint's development. In 1855, Greenpoint was annexed to the City of Brooklyn.

During the 1870s, the shipbuilding industry began to decline because of increasing costs for lumber and the emergence of iron ships. However, this was not the end of industry in Greenpoint. Other industries developed on Greenpoint's waterfront, such as jute mills, oil refineries (Charles Pratt refined

Astral lamp oil), and manufacturing wares, including iron, glass, and porcelain. The growth of these industries brought many Polish immigrants to Greenpoint, since immigration from Poland to the United States was increasing. As migration from Poland was extensive from the turn of the century to around 1930 (Lopata 1976), these individuals are considered early immigrants. Between 1871 and 1890, some 64,776 Poles entered the United States (Lopata 1976). Most of the newcomers were farmers and unskilled laborers, coming from rural areas in Poland. By the turn of the century, Greenpoint was industrialized. The waterfront was lined with heavy industry, and light industry developed in other parts of the community.

Most of the houses presently in existence had been built prior to World War II. While a majority of Greenpoint's housing was built before 1939, many structures were built before 1900. More than 60 percent of the residential buildings are made of wood (New York City Planning Commission 1974). There are a few streets in Greenpoint made up of brownstones and brick townhouses, remnants of Dutch settlement. These particular streets are presently part of a seven-block historic district bordered by Franklin Street, Manhattan Avenue, Calyer, and Kent Streets. Included in this district is the largest collection of commercial structures remaining from the nineteenth century. From the beginning, residential structures in Greenpoint were not taller than six stories, and 71 percent of them contain four or fewer dwelling units per structure (New York City Planning Commission 1974). A small number of housing units were owner occupied, and 81 percent of them were renter occupied in 1980. However, "the percentage of owner occupied buildings with rental units is unusually high" (Wellisz 1982, p. R9). Greenpoint had seen very little new housing, with the exception of some new construction along Mc Guinness Boulevard. Currently, new construction is booming. Few vacant lots have been left unaffected by housing development (with the height and bulk of new housing exceeding that of the community's older housing). In some cases, older, smaller properties adjacent to each other are being disassembled and demolished and larger structures are replacing them.

In 1980, the average median rent of apartments in Greenpoint was $140, while it was $695 in 2000 (Census Bureau 1980; http://factfinder.census.gov). Residents reported that some rents lower than the median existed, usually because of tenure and rent control laws. Along with the city trend, rents in Greenpoint have been escalating. Newspaper advertisements and residents report monthly rents as high as $2,000 and more. In 1983, a sixty-unit apartment building became the first cooperative conversion in the area. In contrast, Greenpoint is now experiencing the emergence of condominium developments through new construction. With the rising cost of land and construction, it is not profitable for developers to build rental housing, since they look to collect their investment and profit quickly. This practice has led to the creation and introduction of condominiums to the New York City housing market.

Brooklyn has been referred to as the "borough of churches," and Greenpoint is a contributor in this regard. There are a number of churches in Greenpoint, "but most with large congregations [are] Catholic" (Susser 1982, p. 35). Catholic churches in Greenpoint served as community centers for ethnic groups. There are two types of Roman Catholic churches in Greenpoint, diocesan and national. Diocesan churches are members of the Diocese of Brooklyn and have territorial boundaries or parishes. The boundaries of diocesan churches do not overlap with each other. National churches are those that serve a particular ethnic group. They usually extend beyond the boundaries of diocesan churches. The national churches offer mass in their national language (Polish, Italian) and English. The diocesan church offers mass in English and usually Spanish. The newer gentrifiers, for the most part, are more secular than lifelong and long-term residents and do not participate in the local religious institutions.

SOCIAL ACTIVISM AND COMMUNITY ORGANIZATION

Greenpoint has a long tradition of social activism that was developed and is maintained by a high degree of social capital. The community is home to a multitude of community organizations that include ethnic organizations, block associations, merchant groups, and church affiliations. Owing to the high degree of social capital in Greenpoint, mobilization is not only highly possible but also a likely response to local issues. Any government bureaucrat, developer, planner, and corporate executive attempting business in the community quickly learns that residents will resist or make demands through action, and persist in their struggle. In addition, the community has a history of advocacy efforts, such as antipoverty programs, day care and senior centers, employment programs, addiction and medical services. This section will present examples of the community's activism. This becomes important for a forthcoming discussion on gentrification, which includes waterfront rezoning, its subsequent development plan, and the positions of ordinary residents regarding future development.

Social Space

As various immigrant groups arrived in Greenpoint from different countries, first from Europe, and later Puerto Rico and Latin America, their churches often served as the locus of social gatherings. As mentioned earlier in Greenpoint, Catholic churches were associated with an ethnic group. These churches also had a number of affiliate organizations, such as the Knights of Columbus. In addition to church membership, immigrant groups formed ethnic organizations and benevolent societies. For some in Greenpoint, they remain in existence, such as the Ancient Order of Hibernians and Smolenski Club. Members from each take their place among the marchers in New York City's St. Patrick's Day Parade and Pulaski Day Parade, respectively. These ethnic social clubs also engaged in local politics, doing the grunt work of electoral political machines in exchange for patronage jobs, such as poll worker on primary and election days or various positions in public schools within the district. Since Greenpoint was traditionally a stronghold of the Democratic Party, these local organizations supported the Brooklyn political boss and club. Often, the children of immigrants participated in additional civic organizations, such as the American Legion.

Community Services

When it came to funding for local services, Greenpoint and Williamsburg were typically coupled because together they make up Brooklyn's Community Board 1. Community Boards are the extension of New York City government on a local level. Community Boards make recommendations about their districts to City Hall.

In 1964, President Johnson called for "a war on poverty in America" (Piven and Cloward 1977, p. 270). The war on poverty was waged through local antipoverty programs. In Greenpoint, these service programs were distributed through the Williamsburg Community Corporation. Initially, local citizen groups used federal money to organize against local governments. In reaction, mayors requested that Congress enact legislation that would enable the federal government to fund community groups through local governments. After 1967, community organizations were funded through state and city agencies. Through this funding stream, Greenpoint accomplished the development of youth programs and senior citizen centers.

THE COMPREHENSIVE EMPLOYMENT AND TRAINING ACT

In 1974, the federal government agreed to directly fund not-for-profit organizations to provide jobs in social programs under the Comprehensive Employment and Training Act (CETA). The federal government was attempting to deal with a high unemployment rate through CETA by paying people a wage while they acquired on-the-job training and work experience. This was historic because for the first time, the federal government deemed not-for-profit community organizations as the recipients of CETA grants. A community organization in Williamsburg, with a history of managing grants, was awarded a $3 million contract under the Comprehensive Employment and Training Act, which included 295 jobs. Jobs carrying various responsibilities were distributed to community organizations. In order to award all 295 positions, new community organizations were created. Many new, not-for-profit organizations were created in Greenpoint and emerged for the purpose of satisfying the CETA grant. Although community organizations received jobs, they did not receive any money from the CETA grant for administrative overhead. Most organizations holding CETA jobs ran storefront operations but did not have any funds to pay rent or to buy furniture. These organizations regularly held fundraisers to support their offices.

The CETA grant put in place a network of community organizations with a paid staff to mobilize around local issues. There was a ready-made cadre of community organizations and residents, who were CETA workers, to participate in community actions. Because of this unique position, residents, who were community workers, were able to attend meetings and events focused on community action during the day or evening, represent the organization for which they worked at these gatherings, and get paid for the activity. In addition, the storefronts could be used for meetings and strategy sessions. CETA unified home, community, and work, enabling people to organize around local issues that were important to them. The leaders of CETA organizations and their employees viewed meeting the needs of the community as part of the staff's workload. Furthermore, with an already established tradition of activism in the community combined with the CETA contract, a union was forged that allowed for ongoing strategizing and mobilization around neighborhood improvements.

THE GREENPOINT-WILLIAMSBURG COALITION OF COMMUNITY ORGANIZATIONS

In the mid-1970s, Greenpoint participated in the "Neighborhood Movement" through the creation of the Greenpoint-Williamsburg Coalition of Community Organizations (GWCOCO). As its name suggests, this organization was a consortium of organizations. It capitalized on the existence of CETA organizations and their nucleus of staff willing to work on community issues. In their classic work, *Poor People's Movements* (1977), Piven and Cloward argue that rebellion declines when organizations are formed. GWCOCO differs from Piven and Cloward's analysis in this regard because it was formed for the *purpose* of community activism for local improvements. The founders of GWCOCO were sure to include representation from the many diverse ethnic groups in the community, as well as from community organizations. In this way, people from different cultural backgrounds worked together for their neighborhood.

In Greenpoint, one issue that GWCOCO rallied around was the closing of the local police precinct. On June 4, 1980, an article appeared in the *New York Post* entitled, "City Hall Mulls Plan to Shut 14 Police Stations." This article aroused concern among residents because although it did not cite particular police stations, Greenpoint's 94th Precinct was going to be moved temporarily while the building was rehabilitated. Leaders of the Coalition were suspicious about the city's "real" plans for the 94th Precinct and wondered if it was on Mayor Koch's "hit list." In July, a rally was held in front of the precinct house "to let the Mayor know that he is not going to close down our police precinct" (*Greenpoint Gazette* 1980, p. 1). Another action held later that month confronted an aide to the Mayor with about 400 delegates who had signed pledges from their neighbors, which were collected by dozens of organizations, stating that they would physically occupy the police precinct should the city attempt to close it. Leader after leader rose at the meeting pledging to fight the city and occupy the police building should it close the 94th police precinct. The community had credibility in this regard since it had a reputation for occupation. A firehouse on the Northside, Engine Company 212, was slated to be closed. Organized by a group called People's Firehouse, residents occupied the firehouse for a year until the city agreed to keep it open (it was only recently closed under the Bloomberg administration). After a series of negotiations between the community and the mayor's office, Koch informed the community in a letter that he "has no plans to close the 94th Precinct" (*Greenpoint Gazette* 1980, p. 1).

By the early 1980s, the Coalition was forced to close because of a lack of funding and a related decision of not competing with its member organizations for resources. But the spirit of activism gained from the collective experiences of GWCOCO lives on. From this history, it is evident that Greenpoint has invested in and accumulated social capital based on rich social interactions. Through their shared social history, residents have become politically astute about how to get things done.

More recently, a couple of unresolved community issues are getting attention from power brokers. One has to do with an underground pool of oil within the community stemming from an underground explosion in the 1950s at the local refineries of ExxonMobil. It was only discovered in 1978 (Confessore 2007, p. B1). This oil continues to leak, pool, and seep into the Newtown Creek, making its way into the East River. Toxic fumes evaporate over the spill. For years the community has fought for clean up by the oil companies to no avail. The issue had finally come to the attention of Riverkeeper, an environmental watchdog group. They filed a lawsuit in 2004 against Exxon Mobil on behalf of the community. Recently in agreement is Andrew Cuomo, New York State's Attorney General. He has "moved to sue Exxon Mobil and four other companies . . . to force them to clean up a half-century-old spill . . . and to repair environmental damage inflicted on nearby Newtown Creek" (Confessore 2007, p. B1). It is hoped that the issue will get serious attention. It is also believed that the oil companies will fight back.

Another long-time community problem focuses on the revitalization of McCarren Park swimming pool. The pool was constructed in 1936 as part of the Works Progress Administration and brought summer fun to many residents and summer day camps through the years with a capacity of 6,800 swimmers (Williams 2007, p. B1). The pool was closed in 1984 and sat decaying as New York City endured fiscal crises. Generations of community activists worked toward reopening the pool or reworking its use. In a twenty-five-year plan for a "greener" New York City, Mayor Michael Bloomberg announced plans to renovate and reopen McCarren Park pool. It will be reduced in scale but remain Olympic size. Using a social class analysis, one questions the timing of interest in bringing resolutions to these long-standing problems. Since Greenpoint is undergoing gentrification, it appears that there is presently a commitment to deal with its pollution and decaying amenities for the affluent and thus add to the community's potential in attracting this same "class" of residents.

NEW RESIDENTS, NEW ORGANIZATIONS

As gentrification continues to increase in Greenpoint, more community organizations are formed. It is interesting that given the vibrant community life in Greenpoint, gentrifiers choose not to participate in existing organizations. Instead, they form their own. For example, one organization, GWAPP (formerly Greenpoint Williamsburg Against the Power Plant and presently Greenpoint Waterfront Association for Parks and Planning), was formed by gentrifying residents to mobilize against the establishment of a power plant on the waterfront. Gentrifiers formed a new organization instead of participating in an established one, such as a block association, church group, or civic organization like American Legion or the Lion's Club.

With each passing day, Greenpoint is more visibly transformed from a bustling working class enclave to a place for the affluent and "creative class."

This transition has had many casualties: the renters who can no longer afford to live in Greenpoint as well as homeowners who have lost these lifelong friends, and who themselves can no longer afford the cost of maintaining property and the general cost of living in New York City, as well as their children who cannot move back home, to the place in which they grew up. It is well on its way to becoming a community that supports a global economy. With economic restructuring, professionals employed by the service economy find Greenpoint quite desirable because of its proximity to Manhattan and other boroughs of New York City, allowing for a shorter commute to work. Additional ways in which gentrifiers are active in the community is the focus of subsequent chapters. The next chapter will present a demographic description of Greenpoint and examine the local forces leading to gentrification.

Chapter Three

Neighborhood Demographics and Change

Greenpoint, like most urban neighborhoods, has undergone change at various points in its history. In part, however, it has resisted change (DeSena 1990; 2005). As I documented in *Protecting One's Turf* (1990; 2005), white residents of European descent reacted to Latinos/as living in the community and attempted to resist their settlement and the in-migration of other minority groups by developing various strategies. One was an informal housing network in which available apartments were rented by "word of mouth." This strategy was an attempt to control who lived in the neighborhood. Obviously, the focus was on the race and ethnicity of potential tenants. To an extent, this tactic was successful since Greenpoint has remained a primarily white community. The latest change that Greenpoint is undergoing is gentrification. How gentrification took hold given the defensive position of this community will be discussed later in this chapter. The chapter will begin with a comparison of the neighborhood's demographics at two points in time, 1980 and 2000. This twenty-year span allows for an analysis of social change leading to gentrification in Greenpoint.

GREENPOINT'S SOCIAL CHARACTERISTICS

Ethnicity and Race

Greenpoint has long been known as a white, working class neighborhood. Since the early 1900s it has been comprised mostly of Irish, Italian, and Polish families. The Irish were the largest group through the 1920s. However, the Irish population has diminished in the community, many of whom have moved to the suburbs. An influx of Polish immigrants arrived in Greenpoint after World War II (Susser 1982). More recently there has been an additional wave of Polish refugees who fled martial law in Poland during the early 1980s. Ethnic segmentation carved up Greenpoint. The different ethnic groups clustered around the churches. For example, the Irish lived around St. Anthony-St. Alphonsus, while the Italians surround Our Lady of Mt. Carmel, and the Poles cluster around St. Stanislaus Kostka and Sts. Cyril and Methodius. Most areas in Greenpoint, however, are heterogeneous.

In 1980, the population of Greenpoint was approximately 39,310 (U.S. Bureau of the Census 1980). By 1980, New York City was showing a decline in population. Hence, like the population of New York City, Greenpoint's also declined. In 1980, residents of non-Hispanic, white ethnic groups made up 75 percent of Greenpoint's population. Since 1950, northern Greenpoint has seen an influx of Hispanic (a Census Bureau category) residents, who in 1980 comprised 21 percent of the neighborhood's population. In 1980, Puerto Ricans were the largest Hispanic group in Greenpoint (63 percent of Hispanics). The remaining 4 percent of Greenpoint's population was made up of Asian (2.5 percent) and black (.50 percent) individuals. One percent identified themselves as "other." Thus, in 1980, 75 percent of Greenpoint's population was made up of whites (non-Hispanic), while the remaining 25 percent was made up of minority residents.

Education

In 1980, 44 percent of Greenpoint's population was high school graduates. The proportion of graduates in Greenpoint was much lower than that of Brooklyn as a whole and was substantially lower than the proportion of high school graduates in New York City. In 1980, 61 percent of New York City residents were high school graduates.

Income

Average median family income in 1979 in Greenpoint was $14,464.00. It was slightly lower than the median family income for Brooklyn, which was $14,664.00 in 1979. These are lower than New York City's median family income: $16,818.00 in 1979.

Occupation

In 1980, Greenpoint residents held a variety of occupations. The largest group was in technical and sales occupations (32 percent), followed by operators and laborers (28 percent) and service occupations (16 percent). Only 9 percent of

Greenpoint's residents held professional or managerial occupations in 1980. This was a substantially lower proportion of professionals and managers than lived in the borough as a whole. In 1980, 21 percent of Brooklyn's residents were professionals or managers. The proportion of Brooklyn residents who held technical and sales occupations (40 percent) was also somewhat higher than in Greenpoint.

A majority of Greenpoint residents (86 percent) were employees of the private sector in 1980, while 11 percent were government workers. The remaining 3 percent were self-employed. This differs from the borough as a whole. In 1980, 76 percent of Brooklyn residents worked in the private sector, 20 percent were government workers, and 4 percent were self-employed. A larger proportion of Greenpoint residents were employees of the private sector than Brooklyn residents as a whole, while a larger proportion of Brooklyn residents were government workers.

GENTRIFYING GREENPOINT

In 2000, along with trends in the city and the borough of Brooklyn, the total population of Greenpoint increased to 47,881 since 1980 (U.S. Bureau of the Census, Tract Data 2000). In contrast to New York City as a whole and the borough of Brooklyn, there were few changes in the racial profile of the neighborhood since 1980. In 2000, 74 percent of the population was white, 2 percent was black, 4 percent was Asian, and 20 percent was Hispanic/Latino/a. Since 1980, there was a 1 percent decrease in whites, a 1.5 percent increase in blacks, a 1.5 percent increase in Asians, and a 1 percent decrease in Hispanic/Latinos/as. In contrast, both New York City and the borough of Brooklyn lost more significant amounts of white, non-Hispanics between 1990 and 2000 than Greenpoint (New York City Department of City Planning 1990 and 2000 Census). In terms of the formal education of Greenpoint's residents, in 2000 those with bachelor's degrees or higher amounted to 31 percent of the population. This is a dramatic increase since 1980. In 1999, the median household income in Greenpoint was $35,435. In terms of occupation, in 2000, managers and professionals constituted the largest group (34 percent), followed by sales and office occupations (19 percent). This is in contrast to 1980 when the largest occupational group was in technical and sales followed by operators and laborers. The persistence of a mostly white community, coupled with an increase of formal education and income among the population and a shift to significantly more professionals and less laborers than in the past, are indicators supporting the development of a gentrifying neighborhood.

In terms of housing in 2000, 81 percent of households in Greenpoint are renters, and about a quarter of these are not rent regulated (Scott 2003). "The percentage of affordable housing in Greenpoint is dropping faster than it is in New York City as a whole. The percentage of rental units in the most expensive category is skyrocketing" (Scott 2003, p. 7). The notion of affordability is calculated as being no more than 30 percent of a household's income going toward rental costs. In Greenpoint in 2000, "about 40% of households paid more than 30% of their income on rent" (Scott 2003, p. 9). The median contract rent in 2000 was $629 compared to $140 in 1980. Market rate rents for a two-bedroom apartment in Greenpoint in 2002 ranged from $1,500 to $1,900 (Scott 2003, p. 160). This represents a 50 percent increase since 1997. Additional indicators of gentrification within the housing sector are featured in articles in the local newspapers discussing "skyrocketing rents" and "loft regulations urged" (*Greenline* 2001). Houses are selling for $600,000 and upwards.

CONDITIONS LEADING TO GENTRIFICATION

Since the 1970s there had been speculation that Greenpoint was ripe for gentrification. This was based on its geographic proximity to Manhattan, its social organization as a community with a high degree of social capital, relatively low crime, an aging housing stock that was attractive and had aesthetic promise, and its relative affordability within a global city. For some local "analysts" familiar with gentrification in other parts of the city, Greenpoint was a "sleeper" waiting to be awakened. What forces led to its stirring? The process of gentrification probably began in Greenpoint in the 1970s by a few "pioneers" who rented an affordable apartment, or purchased a relatively inexpensive house, or even ventured into "loft living" (Zukin 1982), occupying raw, industrial space in mixed-use buildings. With economic restructuring, increasing deindustrialization, and a "rallying" stock market in the 1990s, there was a resurgence of corporate investments in American cities, like New York, and more jobs became available for members of the gentry. "In the long run, economic institutions establish the conditions to which gentrifiers respond" (Zukin 1987, p. 144). In addition, Greenpoint had an emerging reputation as a relatively affordable, "folksy" place to live as members of the young, urban, middle and upper middle class finished college and/or graduate school and began careers. Moreover, as Manhattan and other gentrifying neighborhoods in New York City became too expensive, young professionals looked for other "unclaimed" and more affordable places in which to take up residence. Many came to Greenpoint.

PUTTING GREENPOINT ON THE MAP

Some resident homeowners of Greenpoint were interested in attracting gentrifiers to the community. They had a self-interest in increasing their property values and in the development of local amenities that were more varied than those already in existence. Their strategy was to make Greenpoint visible and to attract relatively more affluent groups than Greenpoint's working class to the neighborhood through historic preservation. On the one hand, this approach contributed to defending Greenpoint from racial change. On the other hand, these homeowners were attempting to contribute to the process of gentrification. A small group of resident homeowners organized an application to the New York City Landmarks Commission. In September 1982, the Greenpoint Historic District was designated and includes approximately seven streets of mostly residential and some religious and commercial structures. Landmark designation attempts to prevent buildings from being altered in ways other than to restore the original façade of the structure (as original as can be located in historical records). The Landmarks Commission was developed as a reaction to the destruction, modernization, and urban renewal in New York City led by Robert Moses. The demolition of the original Pennsylvania Station in New York is often cited as the case that turned the tide of public opinion from accepting a policy of land clearance to one of protection and preservation of history and architecture. In Greenpoint, the protected buildings date back to the mid-1800s, with many architectural styles including brownstones; brick row houses of various sizes, some with glass storefront facades; wood frame attached and semiattached houses; and brick and stone religious buildings. Landmark designation has succeeded in attracting gentrifiers as homeowners and renters.

GAINING ACCESS

In a previous study (DeSena 1990; 2005), I investigated and analyzed the strategies used by Greenpoint's white residents to resist neighborhood change. For the most part, they contribute to residential segregation by race through the development of tactics in which apartments are not rented nor houses sold to people of color. The preference of white residents, in general, is for whites and Polish immigrants over Latinos and African Americans. Given this defensive position, the attempt by residents to control who lives in the neighborhood and the success at preventing racial change, one must ask, how did gentrifiers gain access to the neighborhood? I will present a number of explanations.

Sponsorship

Some studies indicate that the gentry reshuffle from other parts of the same city and are urban dwellers rather than suburbanites (Laska and Spain 1980; Marcuse 1986; LeGates and Hartman 1986). The prior residence of gentrifiers in Greenpoint may have been another neighborhood in New York City, but many had originally migrated to New York City from urban and suburban areas throughout the country. Their initial move to New York was for college, graduate school, and/or work. These experiences served as "urban conditioning" (Fava and DeSena 1984) for life in "the Big Apple." Most were introduced to Greenpoint through a social network, such as a friend or acquaintance who was already a resident, a work relationship within the community, or learning of the community's relative affordability, safety, and charm.

As was indicated in an earlier study (DeSena 1990; 2005), one way that people gain access to housing in Greenpoint is through sponsorship. As previously described, sponsorship is done through a recommendation by a resident to a homeowner on behalf of an individual or family. Through sponsorship people from outside the neighborhood can gain access to housing that is not readily visible or available. It is also a way for those who do not fit the preferred profile of residents (race, age, gender, social class, living arrangement) to gain entry. Thus, initially gentrifiers were sponsored by locals.

Loft Living

Another way that gentrifiers came to inhabit Greenpoint is by renting vacant factory lofts, which for the most part line the waterfront of the East River and Newtown Creek. These lofts constituted empty spaces and served as reminders of a time when bustling factories were the backbone of New York City's economy and their eventual decline through deindustrialization. Loft living enabled people access to the neighborhood initially through raw, industrial space that was not previously occupied for residential living. Many people entered rental agreements knowing that their occupancy was illegal and that they could, at any time, be evicted. Pioneers of loft living in Greenpoint, as in other neighborhoods like SoHo described by Zukin (1982), invested their own money to make the space livable, knowing that their investment could be lost. For many, the risk was worth it given the larger amount of space that one could acquire for the price as compared to a rental apartment. Initially, occupants of lofts in Greenpoint were an assortment of "creative" people who used the space exclusively for work or used it for both work and living. Loft dwellers add to the population of Greenpoint by inhabiting space that had previously been uninhabited and lying dormant.

Race as a Master Status

In *Protecting One's Turf* (DeSena 1990; 2005), white residents of Greenpoint were engaged in "doing segregation" on an ongoing basis in their everyday lives. They defended the neighborhood through their activities. They were particularly attentive to defending against racial change. They were engaged in an "everyday form of whiteness" (Bush 2004) in which white, racialized views directed their daily experiences. This action was taken first by white English speakers and was transferred to Polish-speaking groups.

By treating race as a master status and thereby focusing on the racial characteristics of potential residents, gentrifiers gained access to Greenpoint as a place to live, because as a group, they are mostly white.

As one gentrifier explained,

> I was thinking of the gentrification [here] compared to gentrification in other neighborhoods in the City, which often is maybe like white, artist, YUPPIE types moving into what had been either black or Hispanic neighborhoods . . . like our neighbor . . . she and a lot of her cronies were kind of thrilled by the influx [of gentry] because they were like, "as long as it's not blacks or Hispanics." I mean just blatantly racist about it. But they're thinking, "Well someone's going to come up here and gentrify, and I'm glad it's white people." I think that's why it hasn't been an angry gentrification cause the Polish people, they feel okay about the skin color issue.

Gentrifiers were acceptable to residents because they "fit" the neighborhood's racial expectations of homeowners and tenants. This view was held by multigenerational whites (non-Hispanic) and was extended to Polish-speaking groups. The previous quotation illustrates Cybriwsky's study of Fairmount, a neighborhood in Philadelphia (1978), in which he argues that an alliance occurs between the gentry and white working class residents based on racial prejudice. Thus, long-term homeowners have decided to "let the gentry in" because as a group, they are mostly white. Ultimately, this decision does not support the interests of long-term residents in that there is fierce competition for housing, and renters from all groups are being displaced by more affluent gentrifiers.

Unlike other communities in which gentrification is discussed as a "class war" (Smith 1996) with local resistance (Robinson 1995; Young and Christos-Rogers 1995), the transition in Greenpoint has gone rather smoothly. As one woman gentrifier expressed,

> When I lived in Carroll Gardens there was much less crossover between the Italian families that had been there for generations and the new groups of YUP-

> PIES coming in. There's more crossover here. I feel like there's less conflict of values. I feel like people who had grown up here, been here for generations, Polish families, actually seem to welcome new people. That's my experience. I didn't get the sense that there was any feeling people were threatened, that their territory was being taken. It seemed like people were happy that there were more people coming in. Maybe it's partly because there's a larger Polish group that owns the buildings so there's not a fear that they're going to be pushed out. I think it's a little different . . . if families don't own and then the rents get jacked up so high, and they actually can't live there anymore. I don't think that's the case so much so there's less of a threat.

Gentrifiers are able to spend more on housing than working class and low-income residents. With gentry interested in living in Greenpoint, long-term homeowners were able to raise rents and the price of homes to a potentially lucrative level (particularly for those who inherited their homes from family members and were not holding mortgages or had paid off mortgages).

Thus, for Greenpoint's long-term homeowners, gentrification initially represented a positive change for the community. It appeared that their defense against racial change was successful. Nonetheless, the community never guarded against neighborhood change by social class, particularly the influx of people from affluent and elite classes. Long-term residents probably never realized that as gentrification increased, they would no longer be able to compete with gentrifiers in the housing market. Hence, they are unable to afford to live in the neighborhood in which they spent all or most of their lives. This has mostly been the case for lifelong renters. It is evident by this analysis of Greenpoint that gentrification is a major threat to the future viability of ethnic, working class, and low-income neighborhoods.

Chapter Four

Gentrification in Everyday Life

Everyday life is embedded in the field of sociology. The concept of everyday life is used to elucidate our taken-for-granted interactions and the social life in which we engage. The investigations of contemporary theorists such as Robert Park, Erving Goffman, and Dorothy Smith are grounded in everyday life.

As head of the Sociology Department, Park's vision for the Chicago School was to study the everyday life of various groups and people in the city (1925). Goffman (1959) viewed our actions in everyday life in one sense as theatre, in which we are front stage or backstage engaging in public or private behavior. Public behavior is for an audience, while private behavior involves being oneself. Goffman refers to the "face work" that we do in order to "save face." It involves the work of deference for the purpose of impression management, adjusting one's behavior in order to control the impression one makes on others.

Smith's standpoint theory (1987) focuses on the everyday life of women. Unlike Smith's contention, gentrification in everyday life in Greenpoint does not focus exclusively on women. The accounts of everyday life in Greenpoint lead to an analysis of social class from the standpoint of the working class, including women, who serve as the subordinate group.

This chapter focuses on the interactions of everyday life between ordinary, working class people who are established, long-term (even lifelong) residents and new gentrifiers. Haywoode, in her work on working class feminism (1991), adds another "stage" to Goffman's analysis; that is, community. Haywoode argues that community is located between public and private. Community serves as a middle ground in which the private home and public world meet and social expectations are negotiated. Using Haywoode's conception of community (1991), my focus on everyday life investigates the informal interactions among neighbors and residents of the community that take place on the street.

This chapter documents various clashing social norms between ordinary residents and gentrifiers that get manifested while living together sharing a neighborhood. The aspects of everyday life examined include bicycle parking, housing prices and aesthetics, reactions to noise, and dog walking. This chapter indicates that as newcomers to the community, gentrifiers exhibit a lack of deference toward established ways of life.

BICYCLES

With an increase in gentrifiers comes an increase in bicycle use as a means of transportation within the community and the City of New York. Gentrifiers use bicycles far more than other groups in Greenpoint. One observes gentrifiers riding all types of bicycles, in various sizes (some with decorative baskets), with or without protective helmets, moving in tow with vehicular traffic. Car drivers and pedestrians need to exercise more caution since bicyclists ride both ways on one-way streets. In fact, on one street corner in Greenpoint stands a white-painted bicycle chained to a pole. This white bike signifies that a cyclist was killed on that street. A plaque attached tells the story of a young woman killed by a truck. Negotiation is required for all moving transport vehicles and pedestrians. One lifelong resident said as she crossed the street and was almost hit by a moving bicycle, "These bicycles, they're so arrogant!"

The parking and storing of bicycles by gentrifiers ignites a clash of social norms in Greenpoint. Bicycles are often parked by attaching them to a pole by a chain and locked and left that way on someone else's property. Long-term homeowners often leave notes on these bicycles asking that they be removed and not parked there again. When the bicyclist does not respond to the request of a homeowner, the local police are called to remove the bicycles. The police are able to intervene in these matters because the bicycles are usually chained to a pole indicating parking regulations, so the bikes have become an obstruction to public property. In this vein, I have observed signs on the entrance to subway stations indicating that chaining bicycles to the subway structure violates the law.

The clash exists because long-term residents do not act in the same way. For them, bicycles, including those belonging to children, are stored inside one's home, apartment, or some other place on one's own property. Long-term, resident homeowners are not happy to have bicycles, which do not belong to anyone in their building, parked on their property. As one person said, "If someone trips over it, you're responsible. You'll be sued!" Homeowners perceive these acts as a violation of existing practices and social norms. The following accounts illustrate the conflict between long-term, resident homeowners and gentrifiers over bicycles. One elderly woman resident homeowner explained,

> I came out the other morning and there was a bicycle chained to my pole. My son was over when the owner came back. My son told him not to park the bicycle there anymore. The man started yelling that he could put his bike anywhere he wanted to and said he was reporting us to the police for harassment. He left to go to the police station. When he came back, he apologized and told me that the police said I was right, he couldn't leave his bike near my house.

This account illustrates condescension conveyed by gentrifiers toward requests made by homeowners regarding existing practices. In another instance, a resident homeowner said,

> A few times there have been bicycles chained to the pole in front of our house. They're sometimes there for days. The first time, we thought it was being parked for the winter! My neighbors told me to clip the chain and throw the bike away, but I wasn't comfortable doing that. So I called the Community Relations Officer at the precinct who I knew, and asked if I could get rid of the bike. He told me not to touch it. He took my address and put me on a list at the precinct to have it removed. The police will confiscate them. Another time, there were two bikes left. My wife put a note on one saying that if they weren't removed, we will have the police take them. A couple of days later, my neighbor told me that late at night a car pulled up, two people got out and unlocked the bikes. One read the note and started cursing like crazy. They put the bikes in the trunk of the car and drove away.

Embodied in this narrative is the depiction of clashing cultures stemming from class struggle. Ordinary residents attempt to preserve their way of life, while gentrifiers seek to change those ways or local culture to suit their own lifestyle.

The following exchange occurred between a resident homeowner and a resident member of a local synagogue. The synagogue was located across the street from where the homeowner lived. The congregant said, "I was thinking about putting up a sign saying people can lock bikes on the synagogue gate." To which the homeowner replied, "That's good because I don't want them in front of my house!"

The member of the synagogue is a gentrifier who joined the congregation upon moving to Greenpoint. His position on bicycle parking differs from that of long-term homeowners since he sides with those more like him. Besides, the synagogue is not his personal property, so his decision does not affect him directly.

NOISE

Greenpoint is usually a relatively quiet place, but it is also part of "the city that never sleeps." Thus, on occasion, there is street noise: people shouting, loud parties and music, car horns and alarms blaring, fireworks, bottles smashing on the ground, and the sirens of emergency vehicles. For the most part, these events are treated as background noise. Sometimes, residents will respond to the noise to see if anything extraordinary is happening. The focus here is not on these extremely loud street noises, but on noise associated with everyday life, such as people talking, spending time outdoors, babies crying; noises that are generally perceived as "normal." With the mixing of gentrifiers and ordinary people, there are different perceptions and levels of tolerance for the clamor of everyday life.

One reaction to noise involves a young, working class woman who grew up in Greenpoint and currently resides in her childhood home with her husband and young children. Her next door neighbors are new gentrifiers. She shared the following interaction:

> When [my son] was a baby, he went through a period of night tremors and screamed all night. My neighbors left a nasty note saying that his screaming disturbed their sleep and maybe we should move his room away from [the common wall near] their house.

Another occurrence involved an exchange between a working class resident and a new gentrifier. This was regarding a car alarm.

> My husband leaves for work early and he accidentally set off his car alarm. A neighbor came out yelling, "What are you crazy!" My husband thought he was yelling, [because he was] thinking that someone was breaking into our car. So my husband yelled, "It's fine." But he continued to scream, "Are you crazy, we're trying to sleep!"

Street noises like car alarms disturb everyone. They are part of the soundtrack of city life. The interesting part of the last quotation is that initially, from a working class perspective, the neighbor's yelling was thought to be about protecting another's property and not a matter of noise control to be executed by neighbors.

FILMMAKERS

Greenpoint has become a popular place in New York City for filming movies and television shows. In addition to commercially produced films, independent filmmakers are also found. Commercial filmmakers are required to secure permits and post notices in the community of their forthcoming work in order to reserve parking on local streets for their equipment. Independent filmmakers are smaller operations with fewer people and often impose themselves on the ordinary landscape. I was told the following:

> One resident was visiting his mother who also lived in Greenpoint. He was talking to neighbors as they went by. At the same time, a film was being shot at a house nearby and the man was asked, "please be quiet while we're shooting." The man responded with sarcasm, "You mean when you're done we can resume our normal lives?"

This interaction conveys the tension that exists in everyday life between ordinary people and the new "hipsters" in Greenpoint.

In a similar exchange, gentry impose on gentry.

> A gentry couple explained how they were barbecuing in their backyard and their neighbors, another gentry couple, asked them to please be quiet while they were filming.

They described the situation to me in a sarcastic and humorous manner while at the same time asking, "Can you believe this?"

All these cases bring to light the different meanings attached to living in a community by social class. Working class residents live in a community, which requires cooperation and negotiation, and the reward is mutual concern and assistance. New gentrifiers expect accommodation for their lifestyle and seek to impose their desired lifestyle upon the existing community. New gentrifiers do not look to "fit in" to Greenpoint, but instead, they attempt to take over.

DOG WALKING

Dogs have a prominent place in Greenpoint. They serve as family pets as well as security systems for homes in lieu of alarms. Dog walking is very much a part of the neighborhood culture. Residents are required by New York City law to keep dogs on leashes, "curb your dog," and "pick up after your dog," or face a fine.

Dog walking is another area of everyday life in which new gentrifiers expect accommodation and convey entitlement and superiority by violating the law. Gentry residents walk their dogs on the sidewalk instead of in the street and allow their pets to urinate on trees and the iron gates in front of people's homes and drop their "poop" on the sidewalk. They do not "curb their dog" as is customary in the neighborhood, and often do not "clean up" after the dog.

In some cases, homeowners have installed fencing around trees to discourage dogs and their owners. When abuses are witnessed, long-term homeowners confront violating dog walkers and articulate the local practice as well as the city's law. The actions of new gentrifiers suggest that neither local practice nor city law applies to them.

Resident school personnel, who greet children and parents each morning at a local school, have also expressed concern about the dog-walking style of gentrifiers. The relatively few gentry children who attend this particular public school in Greenpoint are often accompanied by a parent and a dog to the school's entrance. One school aide said, "I told the principal about these dogs. God forbid a kid is bitten. You never know, they're animals!" In addition, there are notices taped around light posts outside the school indicating city laws regarding dogs. The first reminds the public that dogs must be on a leash and the second states the "pooper scoop" ordinance in which there is a fine for not cleaning up after your dog. The location of these notices directly around the school seems like a deliberate reminder to parents with dogs and dog walkers in general.

The everyday life of ordinary residents in Greenpoint has been disrupted by increasing gentrification and the subsequent lack of gentry adaptation to sharing a community with others.

HOUSING

Among Greenpoint residents, it is common to hear and participate in conversations regarding housing. The topic will cover a wide range of inquiries from who has new tenants, who is renovating and/or selling, to the condition of houses and apartments, the amount of market rents, what sold and for what price. In the course of these conversations, the dissimilar interests of working class residents and new gentrifiers emerge. One illustration is a conversation between a lifelong resident homeowner and a gentry resident homeowner who live on the same street. They were discussing a house that was being sold with an asking price of $1.4 million. The gentry homeowner remarked, "I can't believe it's only $1.4 million." The lifelong resident responded, "I can't believe the price either!" The interest of the gentry homeowner is for booming real estate prices, giving her investment more worth. The comment by the lifelong resident was a statement that she could not believe a house in Greenpoint would ever cost that much money.

Another place that differences surface is with regard to aesthetics. The local practice has been to maintain houses in practical ways using materials that are effective and cost efficient, but not always beautiful. The gentry are more interested in aesthetics and support the idea of historic preservation through restoration to original façade. The following dialogue highlights this point:

> A couple stopped to examine and admire the wood shingle of a newly restored home in the historic district. The owner noticed them and came out. They talked for a while about the renovation and the owner remarked, "You don't live in the historic district, so that's good." To which the response was, "Why is that good?"

This exchange presents a number of things. It indicates support by gentrifiers for the aesthetics achieved through historic preservation and restoration. There is also an acknowledgement that there is more social status and economic value in places designated "historic." It is the preferred residence of the gentry. For the resident homeowner, living outside the historic district gives one more options regarding renovation and its cost. In historic districts, rules designated by the N.Y.C. Landmarks Commission limit one's choice of building materials, color of the building's exterior, and stipulates an approved architectural plan and a permit. Approved restoration is a relatively costly endeavor. Once again, the different standpoints regarding housing costs, location, and appearance are brought to light and provide an additional layer to the meaning of gentrification in everyday life.

Everyday life in Greenpoint involving the ordinary, working class and gentrifiers defies Goffman's contention that we look to manage the impressions that others have of us. It is logical to expect that gentry newcomers would attempt to make "a good impression" on long-term residents. Instead, gentrifiers assert themselves in order to create "a definition of the situation" in an attempt to colonize working class life. Gentrifiers do impression management with each other and proceed to make their ways of everyday life dominant in the community.

It is within this context that local institutional arrangements develop. They are the focus of subsequent chapters.

Sewer Treatment

Youth Soccer

Portal to McCarren Park Pool

Waiting for the School Bell

Hollywood Comes to Manhattan Avenue

Bicycle Parking

Coming Soon: A Room with a View of Manhattan

Little Poland in Brooklyn

A New Service

New Condominiums

Chapter Five

Gentrification and Local Schools: Women Shape the Urban Landscape

This chapter focuses specifically on the effects of gentrification on local schools. This aspect of neighborhood life and the interaction (or lack thereof) between gentrifiers and long-term residents documents the strategies used by gentry families to gain admission of their children to public schools outside the neighborhood. This behavior is in contrast to working class and lower income residents whose children attend local schools. Gentry families overwhelmingly reject local schools, both its physical and social space; thus, they reject a portion of the community. Neighborhoods serve as a microcosm in which the interaction of physical space and social space is played out and reflects the social, political, and economic dynamics of society. For the most part, people share space in neighborhoods. They share various components of the built environment, which fosters social groupings to create, maintain, and change both social and physical space. Local institutions are examples of community space in which schools, houses of worship, recreational facilities, commercial organizations, political clubs, and retail establishments interact with residents to form a place. However, "space is not only relational, but also hierarchical" (Zukin 2002, p. 346). The rejection of social/physical space by gentry families creates a dynamic whereby social relations between gentrifiers and lower income residents are segregated and stratified.

This chapter is also informed by feminism. Feminist analyses have reconceptualized activism as political behavior. The women who participated in this study are engaged in informal and formal activism as they negotiate the New York City public school system on behalf of their children. They do not, however, view their behavior as political. They see themselves acting as mothers, "doing just what needed to be done" (Naples 1991).

A version of this chapter appears in the *American Behavioral Scientist* 50: 241–57.

Data for this chapter were collected through participant observation at playgrounds, birthday parties, play dates, and a preschool in Greenpoint for three- and four-year-olds in which my older son was enrolled. This chapter developed as I took my son to and from school each day and learned that most of the older siblings of children attending the preschool were enrolled in public elementary schools outside of the community. I then documented that in 1998, out of twenty-one children enrolled in the half-day class, ten moved on to prekindergarten and kindergarten programs in public schools outside of Greenpoint, and in 1999, fifteen moved on to public schools outside the community. Only one to two children went on to attend a local school in the community, while the remaining children stayed at the YMCA preschool for another year (since they were too young for kindergarten). All of the other students registered in schools outside of the community. Observations occurred here on a regular basis between 1997 and 1999. For the most part, my observational style was unobtrusive in that I listened closely to the daily conversations among mothers and asked questions of them as a "new" mother who was investigating and learning about schools. All of the respondents were women.

FRAMING THIS CHAPTER

This chapter investigates the relationship between the gentry's rejection of local schools, the meanings (Mills 1993) they attach to the neighborhood, and the consequences of their actions on the community.

In addition, unlike most studies on gentrification, this chapter examines gentrifying families with young children who reside in Greenpoint. It investigates the strategies they have developed for negotiating their children's primary education. Furthermore, this chapter examines "women's work" in the process of gentrification, as children and community are designated as the exclusive domain of women (DeSena 1990; Holloway 1998). Thus, the social milieus of children and community are gendered. One way that women gentrifiers residing in Greenpoint express their gender and relative social class is by negotiating the system of education for their children. It is typically women who are mothers who serve as the primary caregivers of young children. They are the ones moving about in the community, collecting and disseminating information about programs for children, and organizing events for children. Women use their local networks to investigate matters of concern and use the information to make decisions. These women are engaged in political behavior. Feminists have reconceptualized political behavior to include a much broader collection of activities than participation in the electoral process. Everyday actions are politicized. "Political life is community life; politics is attending to the quality of life in households, communities, and workplaces" (Ackelsberg 1988, p. 308). Feminist analyses indicate that women have mobilized collective actions locally against perceived injustices and for a host of services. The literature documents women as the guardians of neighborhoods working to preserve the physical and social space (Susser 1982; 1988; DeSena 1990; 1994; 2000), fighting against racism (Naples 1998), toxic dumping (Gibbs 1982; Krauss 1993), and organizing rent strikes (Castells 1983; Lawson and Barton 1980). Women are also found shaping urban space through community organizations and working toward improvements in social and municipal services (McCourt 1977; Gittell and Shtob 1980; Luttrell 1988; DeSena 1998; 1999; 2000; Spain 2001). This chapter extends this feminist tradition by examining the way in which women engage in gentrification by researching schools for their children and strategizing around gaining admission of their child (and often children) to the elementary school of their choice.

The few studies on gentrification that mention education as a concern of gentrifiers (LeGates and Hartman 1986), typically discuss the preference for private schools by gentry residents of city neighborhoods and point to the poor quality of city schools as an explanation for this preference. Gentry families either move to the suburbs or pay for private education for their children. Robson and Butler's study of London (2001) contends that

> the significance and role of education in gentrification processes cannot be generalized. What is crucial is the examination of cases, in particular the interaction between local educational infrastructures and the varying middle-class strategies designed to exploit them (p. 72).

In Greenpoint, there are a couple of scenarios regarding the segregation and stratification of children through schooling. In general, there is division between local public education and Catholic school education (since these are the only private schools in the community). Working class and relatively low-income families choose among them. Often, the outcome of this public-private school division in local communities is racially segregated schools in which the children of affluent families, who are primarily white, attend private schools, while those from relatively low-income backgrounds, who are ethnically and racially mixed, enroll in public schools. Social class differences are often translated into racial differences. Currently in Greenpoint, the Catholic schools are experiencing declining enrollments, forcing the closing of one school and discussions of consolidating others. The local public elementary schools are highly regarded from the standpoint of city and state testing. Families are taking advantage of them. One observes racial diversity in the local public schools. Another level to stratification and segregation of children in schools involves gentrifying families. Gentry families remove their children from educational institutions within the community. They do not select either Catholic schools or public schools in Greenpoint. Instead, they select among public schools within the entire city of New York. Thus, this chapter indicates how gentry families in Greenpoint negotiate the public school system and search for "appropriate" public schools for their children.

There are clear social class differences between gentrifiers and long-term residents of Greenpoint. For example, all of the women participating in this study have college or graduate degrees and presently work or have worked in professional jobs. Long-term residents are relatively less educated and occupy relatively lower paying jobs than the gentry. Many lifelong renters are experiencing great difficulty in the housing market. Rents are too expensive, and the demand for housing is great. They are looking in other communities, in some cases suburban communities, where they say they can have more space for their money. As gentrification continues to progress, some gentry "pioneers," especially families, are becoming "marginal gentrifiers" (Rose 1984) and would like to purchase a house, but cannot afford one. They find the price of homes outrageous and are either unwilling to invest hundreds of thousands of dollars in a house or are unable to buy. They, too, are looking elsewhere, and some have already moved to other East Coast cities.

PUBLIC EDUCATION

The system of public education in New York City, the largest in the nation ("Mayor Bloomberg's Chancellor" 2002), is more complex than that of smaller cities and suburban towns. Unlike the suburbs and smaller cities, New York City schools are funded through general revenue from an income tax, not exclusively through property taxes like in the suburbs. Public education in New York City is currently centralized as the Department of Education under the supervision of a Chancellor who reports to the mayor of the city of New York. This represents a reorganization of public education under the Bloomberg administration. This reform includes the dissolution of the Board of Education, district superintendents, and community school boards. The Bloomberg administration claims that this restructuring will allow for more money to be put into the classrooms. Within New York City's system, like in other large cities such as Chicago and Los Angeles, children are expected, for the most part, to attend the elementary and middle schools corresponding to their street address. There are a few exceptions to street designations.

Alternative schools (gifted programs, charter schools, discipline oriented) are available to residents outside geographic boundaries, through an application, test, or lottery process. Moreover, parents can apply for a variance to place their children in a school other than their appointed one. These are granted if there are seats available and for various reasons, such as both parents being employed and the preferred school being in close proximity to a parent's work place. Siblings of children in attendance are also given preference in these schools over first-time applicants. All public schools in New York City are part of the same education system. Thus, within all five boroughs education money remains within the system even when variances are granted.

This chapter discusses the acceptance of local schools by working class and low-income residents and the rejection of local schools by gentrifiers. Unlike Robson and Butler's study of London (2001), in which the dynamics of school selection are examined in two distinct boroughs, gentry residents of Greenpoint use the entire city of New York as a pool of potential elementary schools.

Despite socioeconomic differences within the population of Greenpoint, women's activism is similar. Like their lower income neighbors, women gentrifiers are also active participants in the Greenpoint community. Their concerns are the physical environment, local issues affecting children, and education. For example, gentry women, on behalf of family, have organized around the levels of lead in and around a park and playground stemming from paint chips after the Williamsburg Bridge was scraped and repainted and also from a nearby paint factory, which was demolished. Moreover, they participated in negotiations with the state to determine the best resolution to the loss of trees in the community because of infestation from Asian beetles. Many gentry mothers were involved in the creation of an organization called Park Moms, in which they lobby for improvements and engage in ongoing vigilance of local parks and playgrounds. In some instances, the local concerns of women gentry differ from those of long-term residents. In these instances, each group would form their own organizations and arrange meetings, demonstrations, and events with other families and groups like them. Education is an example of such a difference. Working class and low-income women will use and be active in local schools, while gentry women use and invest their resources in schools outside of the local neighborhood.

ORDINARY WOMEN AND ORDINARY SCHOOLS

As in the previous chapter, I use the concept of "ordinary" to refer to the typical, everyday life of working class and low-income residents of Greenpoint.

These are the people who attempt to work on a regular basis, have little if any disposable income, and maintain a cohesive neighborhood through high levels of neighboring and active participation in community organizations and neighborhood institutions. They lived in Greenpoint and were active in the community prior to gentrification. As mentioned earlier, working class and low-income residents of Greenpoint, for the most part, choose between either local Catholic or local public schools for their children. They do not consider any other options.

For some, Catholic schools are selected because of the teaching of religious values and perceptions of superior quality, more discipline, and safety when compared to public schools. As one mother said about choosing a Catholic school for her son, "The kids are nicer, better behaved [in a Catholic school]."

In some instances, the decision is based on where the children in one's immediate geographic area attend school. "We chose St.________ because that's where all the kids in the neighborhood would go. It was a communal thing for us."

The selection of local public schools is based on perceived quality, more resources in the form of free books and computers, and no required tuition payment. Some residents see the value with no additional cost. Having three children enrolled in a local public school, one woman said, "Why should we pay? Mrs.______ said that St._________ School is terrible now, and she use to teach there!"

Another woman, who presently teaches at a public school but whose four children attended Catholic school, recommended that her sister select public school for her young children. She contended, "I think the public schools are better."

Interestingly, for working class and low-income families, there was no consideration of enrolling children in schools outside the neighborhood. In some cases, residents may be unaware of available alternatives within the public school system. For "ordinary" mothers who know that they can apply, on behalf of their children, to schools outside Greenpoint, the sentiment expressed is, "It's hard to go to Manhattan." These women want to school their children locally.

ACTIVIST MOTHERING AND LOCAL SCHOOLS

A major issue for gentry women, which they encountered first (because as mothers, they are typically on the "front lines"), is their dissatisfaction with local schools. This is not surprising since, as noted earlier, children's intellectual development is "women's work" (Holloway 1998). Although a few of the local elementary schools are highly rated based on citywide and state test scores, and others are academically average, gentry women are critical of them. The local schools are negatively judged because of their traditional approach, including "teaching to the tests." In fact, in 2003, two elementary schools in Greenpoint scored between 90 percent and 95 percent on state tests for fourth graders. In other words, between 90 percent and 95 percent of fourth graders in these schools are performing at or above New York State standards for fourth grade. These schools were released from using a standardized curriculum by New York City's Department of Education. Ironically, they probably had been using a standardized curriculum in order to achieve high scores. If one only considers test scores, some gentrifiers select relatively inferior schools for their children. When asked why a school outside the community where only 45 percent of fourth graders met or exceeded state standards was selected, one mother replied, "We wouldn't even consider that Shaw shank place [a public school in Greenpoint]. I went to a PTA meeting because they don't hold a tour. I snuck in. It was like a prison." This mother viewed her son's assigned local school as too rigid. As this woman indicated, the fact that the schools in Greenpoint do not readily allow resident families to tour them was a concern. Another woman said,

> [The local schools] they don't [hold tours]. I had been calling PS17 . . . because my husband and I wanted to see what's going on. Like what is everyone turning down? There's a pre-school there and I've never seen it. But when I called, I called a bunch of times, and they said to me, "How old is your child?" And I said, "She's almost three." And they said, "Call us back in a year." And I said, "Well I'm really just interested in looking," and I got slammed down. I called like three or four times. Anybody who has a choice, if they think there's a choice, [encounter an attitude] "don't come to our school. Come to us because you're just going to come to this school." I'm seen as an outsider already because I have a choice, because I think I have a choice, I'm seen as an outsider calling the school. That's like a threat to the school. No, I didn't get in [to visit]. Just like parent involvement is not encouraged.

Unlike prior research that indicates the tendency of the gentry, upon having families, to leave city neighborhoods because of the poor quality of public schools (LeGates and Hartman 1986), in Greenpoint, the gentry prefer public education over private education. Catholic schools are not an option because as a group, they are more secular than their lower income neighbors who support the local religious institutions. Furthermore, tuition in private, non-religious elementary schools in New York City can cost as much as $20,000 annually and more. The move away from private, secular schools and toward public schools suggests that Greenpoint's gentry with families have acquired a relatively affluent lifestyle, but they are not wealthy.

A major strategy developed by the gentry in Greenpoint to remedy their displeasure with local schools is enrolling their children in talented and gifted (TAG) programs and alternative education programs in public schools primarily in Manhattan and to a lesser extent, other parts of the city. They have learned to "work the system" to their advantage. Groups of small children and parents crowd subway platforms headed for Manhattan. Car pools of parents and numerous children attending the same school leave various blocks every morning from Greenpoint en route to the Queens-Midtown Tunnel, the Williamsburg Bridge, or the Brooklyn-Queens Expressway and return in the afternoon in possibly a different car or minivan driven by a different parent. To a much lesser extent, another strategy for children's education is home schooling. Parents who select this option believe that they can do a better job educating their children than local schools because a lot of time is wasted in school and they can teach the curriculum in creative ways. For the most part, these are professional families who attempt to function in a traditional way in which a parent stays at home or has the flexibility to work at home or report to work later than is usual, or leave work early, to be available to tend to children's schedules.

The majority of gentry children are admitted to schools outside of their residential district in a number of ways, including a lottery system. Alternative education programs, which take a progressive approach to elementary education (such as Montessori and Waldorf), tend to admit by lottery. There is a preference for this type of schooling by gentrifiers in Greenpoint. If a child is not accepted, they remain on waiting lists and mothers call the schools on a regular basis to keep abreast of their status and express their deep interest in the school. They behave like the proverbial "squeaky wheel," promise to be an "involved parent," and hope their child gets admitted. Another type of admission policy involves testing for a TAG program for a kindergarten class within a particular school. Although kindergarten is not mandatory in New York State, once a child is accepted, he/she is guaranteed a place for the next six to eight years. Thus, many children from Greenpoint were admitted to TAG programs in schools in Manhattan on the proverbial "ground floor." Siblings of children in attendance are given admission priority. If they are not admitted to the school's TAG program, they are accepted into the regular program in the same school. Rudy Crew, the former chancellor of New York City's schools, had proposed changes to admissions requirements for TAG programs. He argued that existing prerequisites were biased against lower income families and by extension, students of color. His contention was based on the fact that one criterion for admission was an evaluation by a psychologist paid by a child's family. Psychologists acquired reputations for this work, and parents would inform each other of the skills that the evaluation assessed in order to recommend a child for TAG. Thus, children were prepared for their evaluations. Given Rudy Crew's shortened tenure as chancellor, his criticisms of admission to TAG were never institutionalized on a citywide basis. Presently, each school district within New York City administers gifted programs with various admission requirements and time lines. In some cases, children living outside of the geographical boundaries of the school district are no longer eligible for TAG programs in another district. Another strategy developed to deal with these changes is described in the following statement, "We'll rent an apartment for a few months in that school's area. Once she [my daughter] is accepted, we'll give it up."

One of the first generations of children from Greenpoint attending elementary school in Manhattan has advanced to middle school and high school. They are attending some of the "best" (Hemphill 1999) public middle schools and high schools in New York City. One questioned how these children were admitted to middle school in Manhattan, since one school official stated that "they had not accepted students from outside their Manhattan district in years." It seems that because the children attended elementary school in the Manhattan district, they were given priority for applying to middle schools in the same district. Thus, one finds that gentry families are quite clever in their approach to schooling their children. In this case, they were "tracking" their children to highly rated schools with their initial kindergarten admission.

THE RIVER SCHOOL

A final strategy that would address the gentry's dissatisfaction with local schools in Greenpoint is the creation of an alternative education program within the community. A group of gentry women have been preparing the required documents necessary for this project. One woman spoke at length concerning the origins of The River School.

> We looked around and saw that our kids have these bonds with the other kids and we have bonds with the other parents. We wanted to have our group stay intact somehow. It would be nice to walk to school and have play dates at each other's houses. We sat around and talked for a long time, talking about the fact, how could we all be in school together? Is there a way we could all be in school in Manhattan at the same place? We didn't like that idea because . . . I don't like the idea of being in Manhattan and then having difficulty with play dates. That was definitely the main drive [for The River School], that we

> wanted to stay together. Of course, that's not the way it's going to happen. I want my children to go to a school that's really part of the community. I don't want it to be this little microcosm of these white families, who have moved in, who started a school. I want it to be part of the community. And it means that there won't be enough seats for everybody in our group in our school. But I wouldn't choose a private school for that reason either, because I don't want my kids to be with only one group. I don't want them just to be with kids who can afford private school.

These women, the planning team of the River School, have collectively written a proposal outlining the theme and pedagogical approach of the program. Decision making was done by consensus. They envision that this alternative education program commence with four prekindergarten classes and two first grade classes, and be housed within an existing public school or other space contracted by the Department of Education within the community. The curriculum will focus on the community and thus, the name, River School, which refers to the East River. This program would take an interactive approach to curriculum and include an enrichment program of music, the arts, and a foreign language. Parental involvement is strongly encouraged. As the previous quotation indicated, the planning team recognizes the benefits of and welcomes integration with working class and relatively low-income residents. In fact, the admissions policy they suggest is a lottery, which would strive for a culturally diverse student body. They realize that given this approach, their own children may not be admitted.

The River School has encountered a number of obstacles and challenges. With New York City's public school system in flux over the past decade, and the more recent termination of the Department of Education, district superintendents, and community school boards, and centralization under the mayor, the River School's fate remains unclear. Regardless, gentry women proceed with their vision and continue in their efforts.

As children near kindergarten age, gentry women visit and apply to a variety of schools within the city. Since the River School has yet to begin, children have moved on to other schools, primarily in Manhattan, and the project of opening the River School has been passed to the next generation of gentry mothers seeking a local alternative for their children. According to a member of the original planning team, the focus of the River School has changed. She noted,

> The people who have moved here recently are very elitist. They don't want their children to integrate [with working class and low-income residents].

This approach contradicts the initial plan to mix children of all backgrounds. The new plan is to overtly divide the community's children. Segregation and stratification by social class is maintained and reproduced by separating the neighborhood's children.

As mentioned previously, feminist analyses would regard the women in this study as "activist mothers" (Naples 1992). They are engaged in political behavior. These women, however, do not see themselves as politically active. They view their community work as "mothering." One woman said,

> I'm not politically active. As a mother I'm working on The [River] School and I think it would be positive for the whole community, but I'm really outside the political realm. I don't follow what's going on.

This analysis demonstrates that through their informal strategies of negotiating the public school system, and their formal approach of attempting to start an alternative school, these women engage in political action. They forge ahead with determination, offering strategies for those dissatisfied with schools in the Greenpoint community.

CONCLUSIONS

This research is significant in a number of ways. The actions of gentry women have consequences for community cohesion. One major consequence of women's work in the process of gentrification is segregation by social class of children within local schools, which are seemingly reserved for working class and immigrant families. This outcome is similar to neighborhoods in which private schools are patronized by the gentry. In both cases, a consequence of gentrification is that the local public schools experience a segregated student body by social class and possibly ethnicity and race by extension. In the aftermath of *Brown vs. Board of Education*, this analysis indicates how the segregation of schools continues and how ultimately, social class privilege is reproduced. The gentry are more accustomed to relative privilege and have made a judgment about what constitutes quality education. Their lower income neighbors accept local public schools and believe that their only other choice is to pay tuition at a local Catholic school. They are largely unaware of the options within the public school system, such as entrance by lottery or applying to specialized schools for music, science, performing arts, etc., and the additional strategies used by their gentry neighbors. These practices result in negative consequences for community cohesion.

One must ask why gentry residents with children stay in Greenpoint given their dissatisfaction with local schools. Many gentry residents moved in as singles and childless couples. Schools were not a consideration. They stay because "the lifestyle for sale is defined by a place—the city" (Mills 1993, p.

154), in this case, New York City. Residential choices were made based on housing options in which space could be acquired for a relatively affordable price. This explains why one lives in Brooklyn instead of Manhattan. These findings raise another question, why do gentry women choose other public schools outside of the community instead of using their many resources, such as their human and social capital, to gain control of local schools and change them to better represent their wishes and lifestyle? A simple explanation is that it is probably easier to commute children to and from school and "work the system" than it is to mobilize change within the New York City public school system. A more meaningful explanation, however, is that school selection is a reflection of the gentry's social status. Their social status as artists and professionals, with more affluence and formal education than their working class neighbors, gets reproduced by sending their children to schools in more upscale places, like Manhattan. In this way, the gentry are "doing" social class and social status. They also live in a trendy, changing community in which they "do cultural work with symbols of working class culture . . . stigma and status" (Mills 1993, p. 158). The stigma is living in a working class place, the status is creating a lifestyle and community within that place.

The findings in this chapter indicate that gentrification in Greenpoint has yet to contribute to public education. Gentry women's consideration and approach to schooling may change given increasing gentrification and reforms to the education system. In other words, as gentrifiers become long-term residents coupled with the massive changes taking place in the New York City public school system, opportunities to alter local schools to better meet the gentry's sense of quality education may be taken advantage of.

Through the informal and formal activism of women gentrifiers who are mothers, the system of education is navigated and negotiated on behalf of their children. It is a "moral geography of mothering" (Holloway 1998). In the process, they are engaged in political behavior, but not a progressive politics. Instead, they participate in segregation. How do women find themselves in this position? Patriarchy relegates this task to them as women and mothers. They do the work necessary to care for their children.

> To do the work society assigns them, women have pursued social rather than narrowly political goals. When it appears that the survival of the community is at stake, women activate their networks to fight anyone—left or right, male or female—whom they think interferes with their ability to preserve life as they know it (Kaplan 1982, p. 566).

The work of gentry women in Greenpoint is no different from the middle class women Brantlinger (2003) studied in the Midwest nor the perceived threats to children in Atlanta examined by Martin (2008). In all cases, the ideology of these women supported the educational decisions they made for their children and the boundary—work in which they engaged.

This chapter also represents one way that social stratification is reproduced by the work of women in the process of gentrification. Through strategies for acquiring a relatively privileged education, social class and social status are maintained. By attending school outside of Greenpoint, the children of gentrifiers are removed from the community. They are separated from their working class and immigrant peers with whom they live. This practice diminishes social integration and the subsequent formation of social networks outside of one's group within the community. The preschool network remains intact in that the children of the gentry socialize in the community with other children who are just like them. In addition, the local community of gentry (parents and children) form friendship networks because children attending specific schools often travel together, have established a youth soccer league and annual parades, a caroling troupe at Christmas, and planting events at McCarren Park. They maintain a cohesive community with each other and are not integrated into the larger, more ethnically diverse community. Gentry children's enrollment at a school in Manhattan or one with a progressive approach, such as the planned River School, serves as a way for the gentry to maintain and reproduce their social status, upward mobility, and empowerment as parents negotiating a global city. Gentry children are taught that they are privileged relative to their working class neighbors. The actions of the gentry contribute to increasing class, ethnic, and racial segregation and stratification, ultimately producing greater social inequality.

Chapter Six

Soccer Moms in the City

This chapter investigates childrearing styles by social class in Greenpoint. Parents' approaches to socialization are examined through the activities of children. The primary distinction is between working class and gentrifying residents, though finer distinctions are also made.

Greenpoint is home to people of a variety of social classes. Residents are poor, working class, middle class, and upper middle class. Among the higher socioeconomic status groups are gentrifiers. Supported by data in a previous chapter, even though Greenpoint has been a working class community for most of its history, Greenpoint's poor and working classes are being displaced by a very expensive housing market driven by gentrification. Some lifelong residents of working class families have achieved middle class status through higher education offered in particular through the City University of New York (CUNY). The CUNY system was conceived with the ideology that higher education was a right, not a privilege, and was, therefore, free to New York City residents. In response to the New York City fiscal crisis, and as a measure of austerity, tuition was instituted in 1975. Members of working class families in Greenpoint took advantage of higher education through CUNY and are now teachers, administrators, and managers of corporations and government agencies. Another type of middle class resident is the small business owner. This group includes relatively recent immigrants as well as long-term and lifelong residents who own and manage local restaurants, medical and dental offices, hair, skin, and nail salons, and other retail and service establishments. This group is relatively financially secure and owners of homes and other properties in the community. They may be similar to the newer gentry class economically but are more vulnerable to higher rents for their retail business establishments if they do not own the building in which their business is housed. They are also more "ordinary" than the gentry.

They are regular, unpretentious people who work hard to raise their families according to traditional values. For example, Greenpoint's middle class, for the most part, remains connected to religious institutions. They may attend services regularly or occasionally, send their children to religion classes, and select religious rituals for births, weddings, and funerals. In comparison, the gentry in Greenpoint are far more secular with little, if any, affiliation with local religious institutions. In addition, the children of middle class residents attend local elementary schools, either religious or public. As indicated in the last chapter, gentry children attend school outside of the community. In some instances, middle class residents "behave" more like their extended working class families and neighbors, while in other cases, they follow the ways of their gentry neighbors. This is also the situation regarding their approach to raising children. Thus, this chapter continues the investigation of everyday life within the process of gentrification by analyzing children's patterns of recreation as an indication of their parents' approach to the process of socialization. In the end, the differences can be attributed to a family's social class, and thus, the lifestyle they fashion based on human capital and economic resources made up of features obtained from their own family experiences while growing up in city and suburban settlements.

Research on children's activities focuses, for the most part, on the relationship between recreation, social, and cognitive development. This literature stems from the work of classic symbolic interactionists such as Mead and developmental psychologists like Freud, Erikson, and Piaget. Mead, in particular, examined differences between play and games in children's development, noting children's readiness to deal with social expectations through games with rules. More specifically, Mead discusses the emergence of the social self through play, game, and the "generalized other" (Mead 1934). According to Mead, toddlers engage in imitative play. As children grow, their "make believe" play indicates the beginning of their ability to "take the role of the other," a necessary component for the development of a social self. At this point, however, children cannot yet manage to assume the role of numerous others. Children eventually reach a point where they can play games involving a set of rules to follow as well as anticipating the actions of other players. For Mead, other people represent the generalized other, the views of society. The social self emerges through interaction and an internalization of the generalized other in which the perspective of society becomes one's own. Through this process, the social self develops.

The analysis of children's play is underrepresented in community and urban sociology. Few community studies explicitly include children (Liebow 1967; Susser 1982; Anderson 1990; 1999). Anderson's study of the "code of the street" (1999) investigates the effects of poverty, violence, and drugs on youth. The bleak future prospects for these children inform Anderson's social policy recommendations (1990). To a large extent, community sociologists have not studied children of varied social classes within the context of a neighborhood. Children are "there" (Lofland 1975) as part of the scene or background, but for the most part, are not included in the analysis. This study on gentrification in Greenpoint places children at the forefront of the analysis. Instead of exploring human development, children's activities are examined as a reflection of social class and their parents' ideologies.

More recent studies examine how children spend their time. Hofferth and Sandberg (2001) investigate children under age thirteen, utilizing data from the "1997 Child Development Supplement to the Panel Study of Income Dynamics" (p. 295). Parents completed time diaries about their children's week. The researchers report that a majority of children spend their time "eating, sleeping or in personal care" (p. 306). This was followed, in order from most to least, by school or day care, free play, television viewing, and other structured activities. They spent little time reading and studying. "Passive leisure," such as art, housework, and talk completed a child's week. This study makes some distinctions regarding family type. For example, children with employed mothers spend more time in day care than children with unemployed mothers. In addition, children from single, female-headed households spend more time in structured sports than other children. In this study, there is no distinction made regarding the type of place in which children are spending their time. In addition, social class is not considered. The researchers miss the broader social context beyond the family of place and class affecting children's daily lives. Options for children's activities differ depending on whether one is living in the city, suburbs, or country. One's social class, as a determinant of parenting styles and economic resources, affects the type and extent of children's activities.

In her book *Unequal Childhoods* (2003), Lareau uses social class as the focal point of her analysis. She compares the practices of middle and upper middle class families with working class and poor families. Her comparison also implies differences between city and suburban settings. She begins by describing two schools that are central to her investigation. One is located in a working class neighborhood within a city in the northeast. This school's population is made up of students from other poor and racially diverse neighborhoods as well. The other school is outside the city in a suburban neighborhood. Lareau's middle and upper middle class families come from the latter.

Lareau argues that the middle class children are raised by a parenting style of "concerted cultivation." Children are enrolled in countless organized activities supervised by adults, and parents transport their children from one place to another. Moreover, parents constantly talk to their children, articulating a model of reason and logic and playing verbal games aimed at teaching and nurturing their verbal skills. These parents are also strong advocates for their children with teachers and coaches, while also encouraging their children to assert themselves. Lareau notes that these middle class families, parents and children, are exhausted from the intensity of their everyday lives. Yet, the children seem to acquire verbal and behavioral skills necessary for a smooth transition into adulthood, equipped with skills necessary to function within social institutions.

The working class and poor children studied by Lareau are reared by an "accomplishment of natural growth." In these families, there is a clear division between adults and children. For the most part, children are expected to play with each other, entertaining themselves without adult involvement. Children are also expected to follow adult directives without argument or verbal banter. Lareau finds that these children seem more imaginative, less tired, and in general, happier than their middle class peers. At the same time, these families were more removed from social institutions and expressed more deference to their agents than their middle class counterparts. Thus, according to Lareau, parenting by the use of concerted cultivation are investments toward the development of human capital in middle class children, thereby giving them an advantage over working class and poor children in an increasingly rational world.

In some ways Lareau's investigation is stereotypical, with the middle and upper middle class living in the suburbs and thus attending a suburban school and the working class and poor living in a city, attending a city school. This chapter focuses on children's play in Greenpoint, a city neighborhood. Social class is at the heart of this investigation as the children of gentrifiers are compared to their working class and lower income peers.

Lareau's analysis also raises the issue of adult supervised activities in the lives of children. She describes how middle class children's lives are directed and negotiated by adults, namely parents, teachers, coaches, and the instructors of enrichment classes. Their lives are greatly organized and scheduled. However, the notion of adult supervision varies even within organized activities.

Chin and Phillips's (2003) study of children's time use makes the point that there are varying degrees of adult supervision in structured activities. In school settings, for example, teachers and staff are not always "present" to direct a child's every movement. Even in organized sports, periods in the locker room and on the field are more informal. Children interact and talk, tease, fight, make friends and enemies.

Gerald Handel uses oral histories of men to present "A Children's New York: Boys at Play in Yorkville" (1984), about a neighborhood on Manhattan's Upper East Side. The men recall how the city was their playground and the East River their swimming pool. Through this study, Handel attempts to combine child development and urban sociology by examining social relations on the street (p. 33). Presently in Greenpoint, one observes both informal play among school-age children "on the street" as well as adult-organized, supervised, and structured recreation in the form of play dates, team sports, and birthday celebrations in "party places." Implicit in a discussion of children's play is the intention of parents who direct that play (either by design, routine, or tradition). In the end, this discussion is about parental ideals regarding their children that originate from one's social class.

ORDINARY KIDS

Once again, the concept of "ordinary" is used here to express that which is typical and has come be the neighborhood tradition created by a local culture. Greenpoint's ordinary kids are from working class and poor families, some of whom are relatively recent immigrants. Most of the American-born children are from families with numerous generations living in the community. They experience generational continuity, inheriting a legacy of community in Greenpoint as their "home."

Children old enough to be outside on their own roam the streets, visiting local establishments like parks, the library, and pizza parlors, using the neighborhood as their playground. They ride bicycles, skateboards, and scooters, play basketball, stickball, handball, and more sophisticated versions of games like tag and hide and seek. Some observers think that these children, who wander the local streets, have nothing to do, but while they are doing "nothing," they engage in verbal exchanges, decision making, problem solving, and endless negotiation. They create and participate in the community.

To an unwitting onlooker, children wandering the streets, changing locales and activities, appear to be unsupervised. For ordinary kids in Greenpoint, that is seldom the case. There are multiple social networks operating in which adults, sweeping sidewalks, hanging or gazing out of windows, or simply passing by, keep an eye on the children. As one resident said,

> I know that [my son's friend] climbs the fences into the abandoned factories. My son knows he better not go there. I tell him, "We're watching."

Interestingly, in this family, both parents work full time. So the idea of "we're watching" is actually a reference to an assorted collective of local family, friends, and neighbors.

Residents will also utilize their relationships when warranted. Children are sometimes confronted directly or their parents are contacted when an incident occurs. One resident explained,

> We were out for a walk and noticed these kids sitting in my wife's car. It was parked near the factory. My brother happened to be approaching us. I signaled to him and we ran toward the car. They saw us coming and got out and started running, but I recognized one of the kids. I went to his house and spoke to his father. They paid us for the broken window.

Ordinary children in Greenpoint have the freedom to explore the neighborhood terrain, while subject to the scrutiny of adults. With the emergence and widespread use of cell phones, there is more ongoing contact with parents. One mother said, "We have him [her son] call in."

Ordinary children in Greenpoint are given the same allowances as their parents were given growing up in the community. They are following the established tradition. One mother remarked, "Groups of us would go camping for days. You want your kids to have experiences in life."

ORGANIZED SPORTS

Another type of activity for ordinary children in Greenpoint is organized sports. Adults and children have mainly participated in two athletic traditions in the community, baseball and basketball.

Baseball

Baseball instruction and play are offered through three community organizations, namely the YMCA, Little League, and Police Athletic League (PAL). The Greenpoint YMCA presents a "Junior Mets" program that is sponsored by the YMCA of Greater New York and the New York Mets. It is free to boys and girls ages five to fourteen during July and August (Greenpoint YMCA, Summer, Fall I, Fall II 2006 Catalogue).

Greenpoint Little League is a major outlet for baseball. This local organization is part of the National Little League Association. In Greenpoint, it is mostly boys who participate.

The Police Athletic League (PAL) also sponsors a baseball league in Greenpoint. Parents who opted for this league over Little League said that "it was less competitive and more instructive."

Basketball

Basketball is offered through two neighborhood institutions. The local YMCA forms teams of "Junior Knicks," which stems from a collaboration between the YMCA of Greater New York and the New York Knickerbockers. Boys and girls ages seven to eighteen can participate in instructional and league play from January to May. It costs $25.00, but is free of charge to those twelve to eighteen years old because of a special grant (Greenpoint YMCA, Summer, Fall I, Fall II 2006 Catalogue).

Basketball is also offered through the Catholic Charities, sponsored by the Catholic Youth Organization (CYO) and organized through Catholic parishes within the Brooklyn-Queens Diocese. Parishes within Greenpoint and some elsewhere with organized teams would compete in basketball. Play takes place in gymnasiums belonging to each church, and some teams travel, constituting "home" and "away" games. Adults volunteer to serve as the parish athletic representative to CYO and coach teams as well as provide set-up, work the clock designating play time, and sell refreshments during games. Officials, such as referees, are paid.

One major participant in basketball, St. Anthony/St. Alphonsus Church, ended its more than half a century of play. One mother, whose children played for St. Anthony's, explained,

> CYO basketball at St. Anthony's is no longer in existence. The Parish Athletic Representative resigned after years of service, and no one came forward to volunteer to take his place. CYO basketball still exists at St. Cecilia's and St. Stan's. Kids can join those teams.

The end of youth basketball at this parish may symbolize the current state of the local Catholic church in gentrifying neighborhoods. About a year later, St. Anthony/St. Alphonsus School was closed because of dramatically declining enrollment. Gentry newcomers used neither the school nor the basketball league for their children.

GENTRY KIDS

Like ordinary children in Greenpoint, the children of gentry families are also seen strolling the streets of Greenpoint, visiting the video store, the library, riding skateboards, and playing kickball. However, local children are segregated by social class. Gentry children play with other gentry children, and ordinary children play with peers like them. On the streets, in the parks, and engaged in more formal arrangements like a local swim club, the children are not integrated with each other in the community. In fact, one gentry mother commented about the children of her working class neighbors, "They are boys in need of supervision!" As was indicated in the previous chapter regarding play, grouping by social class remains intact, and there is no outreach outside of one's in-group.

The children of gentry families also participate in organized sports, but they have not joined a community-sponsored baseball league or basketball team. Instead, their parents have formed the Greenpoint/Williamsburg Youth Soccer League (GWYSL). GWYSL was established in 1999. It originated with a group of gentry families whose children attended the YMCA preschool. These families organized "pick-up games," informal soccer games among the children. From there they researched various leagues and joined the American Youth Soccer Organization (AYSO). AYSO was chosen because of their guiding principles: everyone plays, balanced teams, open registration, positive coaching, good sportsmanship (GWYSL Newsletter, November 2005). On Saturday mornings from September to December, a multitude of children ages four to fourteen, wearing various colored uniforms designating different teams, engage in playing their game of the week at McCarren Park in Greenpoint. For the most part, these are the children of the gentry. One mother expressed,

> It's nice after 6 years; the kids are off in different middle schools but get to see each other in soccer.

In terms of both play and organized sports, gentry children are segregated from their ordinary neighbors.

Compared to ordinary children, the lives of gentry children take them outside of the neighborhood. The previous chapter discussed the schools that gentry children attend, which are outside of the community. There are additional activities that also remove them from the neighborhood, one of which is enrichment classes. In some cases it is to learn a musical instrument, various types of dance, gymnastics, and language and culture. These classes are outside of Greenpoint.

Some gentry families leave the community for leisure on a regular basis and even for extended periods of time. One example is those who own second homes outside of the city and use them on weekends and for vacations. In an attempt to schedule time for two preteen boys to "hang out," a gentry mother remarked, "We're away every weekend and holidays and vacations. And he takes skiing lessons at our other place. He's quite good!" Time for the boys was not scheduled since one was away a lot. Some gentry families pack up in June and leave for the entire summer, returning for the start of school.

One woman explained, "We're leaving tomorrow for this camp. We go every summer. I work while we're there and my children are able to attend free." Thus, through second homes and summers away, gentry families disinvest in Greenpoint and participate in the activities of other communities.

There is a contradiction between the ideology that gentry families publicly present and the ways in which they guide their children. For example, they select a youth soccer league with values of fair and equal play, but those values seem to apply only to their children. Those outside their social class are kept separate, seemingly not good enough for their children. Moreover, the fees for soccer serve to exclude lower income children, costing $70 for early registration and $90 after a certain date. The cost of soccer is higher than other organized sports teams in Greenpoint. GWYSL offers some scholarships, a way to demonstrate social awareness for the needs of other local children. The clear segregation of children by social class in Greenpoint explains why most gentry children are not playing other organized sports or engaged in activity spots, such as playing Yu-Gi-Oh cards or on WiFi with their gaming microcomputers at the local public library. They are simply not participants in the larger community of Greenpoint.

Chapter Seven

Views of Manhattan for Sale: Rezoning for Residential Development on the East River

Greenpoint's waterfront overlooking Manhattan's east side lay dormant for years, quieted by deindustrialization. Brick buildings, some with steel connecting bridges, and a number of piers were left to deteriorate, but they served as reminders of a vibrant past. In some cases, private warehousing companies located on the river closed off public piers to public access. Such action served the public since the piers were dangerously corroded and the city was not about to address it. From the late 1970s through the 1980s, waterfront utilization ideas by residents and plans by the local community board were developed. The community board developed a 197A Plan, which recommended all kinds of benefits for the community to city government in the form of housing, parks, schools, and social services. It was not until a sustained real estate boom in New York City continued into the new millennium and Michael Bloomberg became mayor that Greenpoint's waterfront became a desirable prospect to City Planning and private developers. If sufficiently developed, it could become a lucrative market.

The Bloomberg administration can be characterized by the corporatization of government, which is executed through private development and revenue production. They are brokers of global capitalism. Luxury development, through rezoning, redevelopment, and tax abatements, is believed by this administration to generate all kinds of economic activity for New York City. And much of the way that this administration produces revenue is on the backs of ordinary New Yorkers. For example, under Bloomberg, permits to film movies and television shows are issued regularly. Filming disrupts everyday life for ordinary people in neighborhoods around the city and has no benefits for inconvenienced residents. In addition, the number of parking violation personnel has been increased so that more parking tickets are issued. I have observed a resident who was double-parked in order to unload her car of packages and pets issued a ticket. Moreover, the Sanitation Department rummages through people's trash in search of recycling violations or looks for the violation of other trash collection ordinances (such as putting cans curbside too early). This even occurred the day after Christmas in which most homeowners on particular streets in Greenpoint were issued a violation for failing to recycle holiday wrapping paper. Another Sanitation summons was issued to a family clearing out an apartment of furniture after a family member had passed away. They were given a fine by the Sanitation Department for putting the furniture curbside prior to 5 p.m. the day before their scheduled collection. In the meantime, the homeowner was trying to prepare the apartment for the arrival of new tenants, revenue that his family needed. Furthermore, property taxes for the small homeowner (1 to 3 people in a family) are also regularly increased by an annual mechanism of reassessing the perceived market value of property each year. And even Bloomberg's plan for "congestion pricing," to rid Manhattan of traffic congestion, has been strongly criticized on the grounds that it would greatly affect ordinary, hardworking New Yorkers by charging them for driving to Manhattan. As a resident of Greenpoint commented, "It's all about money! If Bloomberg is so worried about congestion, he should ban ALL cars from Manhattan." In addition, upgrades to the transit system first need to be implemented to prepare for the increased ridership that would occur under "congestion pricing." Finally, although this policy is proposed under the auspices of "A Greener New York City," it is another step toward preserving Manhattan for the affluent and wealthy. Congestion pricing is currently a dead issue. The New York State Legislature would not even take the time to vote on this proposal, since it faced substantial opposition. In the process, Bloomberg's arrogance and unwillingness to compromise resulted in New York City's loss of hundreds of millions of federal dollars for mass transit. In general, this administration acts as a facilitator of private, luxury development as opposed to performing on behalf of working class residents.

The Bloomberg administration has also made a reputation on housing development. In 2002, the Bloomberg administration proposed a housing program for New York City to include "roughly 60,000 housing units throughout the five boroughs over the next four years" (Steinhauer 2002, p. B1). The plan for these units was to incorporate subsidized apartments for special needs populations, residents with a middle income, and luxury market rate housing for the affluent. About 40,000 units would come from rehabilitation under the control of the city's agency for Housing Preservation and Development (HPD). The remaining housing units would be created through private development, with much of it located along the available parcels of waterfront throughout the city. Community Board 1 (Greenpoint-Williamsburg), the entity of city government in local neighborhoods, anticipated an application from City Planning to rezone its waterfront along with adjacent manufacturing parcels that extended in-land. Instead of using the traditional ULURP (Uniform Land Use Review Procedure) committee of the Community Board (which votes on land use), a Waterfront Rezoning Task Force was developed composed of a variety of local residents both working class and gentry, architects and retirees, to examine the city's plan for the community's waterfront. Greenpoint's large waterfront was already a development priority of the Bloomberg administration, since there is little space left in New York City in which to develop new housing and the waterfront consists of huge parcels of land. After this waterfront is committed there would remain very little nonresidential land left to develop. Only "brown fields" (land contaminated by toxins) remain untouched. Previous mayoral administrations were able to transform cheap, abandoned property with little value, using public funds, and develop housing. Now, with land and housing prices in New York City spiraling upward, unwanted buildings for rehabilitation are relatively unavailable. Furthermore, the executive, billionaire mayor, who participates in the perpetuation of global capitalism, saw an opportunity to pave the way for private elites, like himself, and developers to invest in the "New Marketplace Housing Plan." The administration's initial plan for housing was revised by the negotiations around the development plan for Greenpoint's waterfront. The modification arrived at includes a tactic untried in New York City, the creation of affordable housing through inclusionary zoning. This approach has since been integrated into the Mayor's housing plan citywide. This chapter will examine how the plan for Greenpoint's waterfront was developed and the various views and priorities held by those involved. The analysis will be done within the larger context of the political economy.

Scholarship on gentrification has documented many factors or strategies that have assisted in its growth. For example, in some places there is spillover from a neighboring gentrifying community. Historic preservation has also been used as a tool to attract gentrification, and in some cases, large-scale commercial revitalization plans for gentrification are put in place. In a study of "Postrecession Gentrification in New York City," Hackworth (2002) notes that the state drives the process forward in more conspicuous ways than in the past. This is certainly the case for Greenpoint's waterfront. The first hurdle in the process was rezoning the area before it could be open for investment by private developers for residential use. In this study, Hackworth also contends that opposition to gentrification has been marginalized. This is true in Greenpoint regarding total opposition to waterfront development. Large-scale resistance to development was weakened by threats and attempts of locating additional pollution-causing industries in the neighborhood. Ultimately, through a thoughtful reconceptualization of the city's plan and unrelenting community organization, Bloomberg's commissioners were taken by surprise. The Bloomberg administration was confronted by a community destabilized by gentrification; one that was struggling in the face of it. The administration was informed that their plan would only serve to accelerate gentrification in Greenpoint. In fact, after a community rally, an Assistant Commissioner commented to his colleague, an urban planner who was also a former resident of Greenpoint, "Well, they're done now." His statement referred to a rally which he believed marked an end to the community's response. The planner who had more of an intimate knowledge of the community responded, "No . . . they've only just begun!" The administration underestimated Greenpoint's social capital and its tradition of social activism.

THE INFLUENCE OF COMMUNITY CHURCHES

The Catholic churches in Greenpoint have a long history of serving working class residents. For many, the churches are central to life's milestones. People are baptized, attend school, are married and buried all in the same church, or a neighboring one. Through the years, these churches have experienced a crisis of maintenance. There are fewer priests to serve fewer parishioners and less revenue to support church facilities and schools. A number of Catholic churches in Greenpoint have closed their schools in an attempt to contain costs. Another strategy to deal with this crisis is the creation of parish clusters. In Greenpoint, the local Catholic churches are grouped in an attempt to coordinate and plan their work within the community. This local, Greenpoint cluster became involved in bringing multilingual addiction services to Greenpoint, as they witnessed cases of alcoholism and drug addiction coupled with domestic violence. A resident, who was also a parishioner and long-time community activist working in the substance abuse field, assisted the cluster of churches in securing services. When the project was realized, the clergy and the activist decided to continue focusing on community needs. This time, the issue selected was affordable housing, as clergy were confronted with many congregants facing substantial rent increases and displacement.

The Parish Cluster was assisted by a student of urban planning from Cornell University, who carried out a housing needs assessment in Greenpoint. The study documented the loss of affordable housing in the community, a dramatic increase of total family spending on housing, and the purchase of homes in Greenpoint becoming more unattainable (Scott 2003). The Parish Cluster organized meetings inviting community leaders, local politicians, and Community Board members. It is from here that when the Community Board began the rezoning process of the waterfront that the activist who volunteers for the Parish Cluster was invited to work on housing. Subsequently, Greenpoint's Parish Cluster and the adjacent Williamsburg Parish Cluster joined forces to mobilize around securing affordable housing for working class and low-income residents as part of the waterfront rezoning package.

THE REZONING PROCESS

Rezoning land use in New York City is a legal process referred to as ULURP (Uniform Land Use Review Process) that goes through a number of government bodies in New York City for a vote before it becomes law. The first step in the process is that City Planning certifies its rezoning application, which essentially starts the clock on the legal process. The Community Board receives the application for rezoning and has sixty days in which to review it and vote. Regardless of the Community Board's vote, the application or plan moves forward to the Borough President, who has thirty days in which to review the Community Board's recommendation and vote. The application and votes are returned to City Planning, who has sixty days to review recommendations and hold a public hearing. The City Planning Commission votes. The levels of review discussed to this point are advisory. The final vote rests with the City Council, since they are the legislative body of New York City representing residents. Within fifty days, the Council votes to approve, reject, or approve a project with modifications. The mayor then has five days in which to veto a Council vote. Then, within ten days, the City Council can override the mayor's veto with a two-thirds majority vote (Lander 2004, p. 15). A negative vote from the Community Board, Borough President, and the City Council kills a plan.

THE PROCESS IN GREENPOINT

The Waterfront Rezoning Task Force began its work with visions about the potential future of this parcel of Brooklyn's waterfront. They were not against rezoning and development. In fact, prior to the evolution of the issue of rezoning, there had been plans to expand garbage transfer stations and applications to build a power plant on Greenpoint's waterfront. The community was against these possibilities since Greenpoint has its share of environmental problems stemming from industries producing toxins. Therefore, rezoning away from manufacturing and toward residential or recreational use also handled the threat of additional polluting industries locating in Greenpoint.

A member of the Community Board was quoted in a *New York Times* article regarding rezoning and said,

> There's a pretty large number of people in the community that are opposed to anything above five or six stories . . . But 30 years of saying no to housing proposals on the waterfront is what brought us the proposal for a garbage transfer station, which we were very lucky to defeat, and it's what brought us the proposal for the power plant, which we hope to defeat. So I hope people realize that they've got to say yes to something here (Bahrampour 2003, p. B4).

There seems to have been a view among the Community Board and Task Force members that rezoning and development was the "better evil" as opposed to more pollution and disease from heavy manufacturing.

As the Waterfront Rezoning Task Force of the Community Board got underway, it divided itself into various subcommittees. Those most active were focused on: parks and open space, housing, height and bulk (of new residential towers), and economic development (which included industrial retention and jobs). These subcommittees addressed the various interests of the community. For example, within the areas to be rezoned, task force members wanted assurances that new parks would be constructed as well as public access to the waterfront. Others were concerned about the aesthetics regarding new towers and focused on maintaining sunlight and sight corridors from streets in the "older" community near the waterfront. The subcommittee on housing focused on a guarantee of a number of affordable housing units, as well as the creation of antidisplacement measures. The economic development subcommittee had an interest in seeing that existing industry and jobs were at least maintained if not expanded.

In the course of meetings, with reports given from each subcommittee, the chair of the housing subcommittee wanted the Task Force to prioritize the community's needs. He argued that affordable housing should be their first priority. For the most part, the Task Force rejected this position, claiming that all the areas were equally important and affordable housing was just one issue.

AFFORDABLE HOUSING BECOMES #1

Affordable housing emerged as the primary issue of the working class community in Greenpoint, not parks or open space or aesthetics. As one resident expressed, "Aesthetic concerns are a luxury of affluence." The community mobilized through the tradition of the local Catholic churches. The Parish Clusters of Greenpoint and Williamsburg, which constitute seventeen churches, organized their parishioners around the issue of affordable housing. Each church issued tickets to a rally in which they sought to "kick off" or publicly state that the Catholic churches and their congregations, led by the bishop of Brooklyn-Queens, will fight for affordable housing. Over 500 residents were in attendance and were addressed by local clergy, the chairperson of the housing subcommittee of the Waterfront Rezoning Task Force, and local, elected politicians. In general, remarks criticized Bloomberg's "New Marketplace Housing Plan" for insufficient attention to the housing needs of low and moderate income New Yorkers. The rally made clear that,

> Greenpoint-Williamsburg is an economically and ethnically diverse community and a rezoning that creates enclaves for the rich will not benefit our residents. Instead, we need housing that's affordable to our teachers, firefighters, nurses, secretaries, and police officers—the people that make our community work . . . A fair development plan for our waterfront must guarantee affordable housing in a simple way that is profitable for developers and that harnesses the expertise of our community organizations (*The Church's Response to the Affordable Housing Crisis in Greenpoint-Williamsburg* 2004, p. 5).

The community's slogan and chant "40% GUARANTEE" of affordable housing in development evolved from this collective. The keynote speaker for the evening's event was Brooklyn's Catholic Auxiliary Bishop, Joseph Sullivan. Sullivan was well known from his decades of service as the head of Catholic Charities in Brooklyn-Queens. A local newspaper reported of Sullivan's address to the rally,

> "There's a crisis in housing in this city," the prelate thundered to the 800 or so people—middle class, poor, black, brown, white, Latino, Caribbean, Italian, Polish and every conceivable gradient in between . . . This was a night for the people, not the great and grand" (Ryan 2004, p. 1).

This was a power with which the mayor and his commissioners had not planned to reckon. Thus, negotiations about affordable housing end up being between the Catholic Church of Brooklyn-Queens through the Parish Clusters on behalf of the community, and New York City's government bureaucracy, with local politicians on the side of the church and community. The issue of affordable housing took on "a life of its own" and became the major concern of rezoning and redevelopment for the working class and adjacent poor community. Ultimately, the Waterfront Rezoning Task Force was inundated by community voices giving priority to affordable housing, with the churches and local politicians supporting and working toward this end. Open space, parks, and the height and bulk of new towers were and remain subjects of concern to the gentry.

THE PLAN

The original, proposed rezoning plan presented by the Bloomberg administration was rebuked by the Waterfront Rezoning Task Force. First, there was no guarantee of affordable housing units included in rezoning the waterfront or outside the rezoning site within the larger neighborhood. In addition, the plan lacked a statement defining income categories. The plan was also void of provisions, giving priority of affordable housing units to current residents of Greenpoint. The call by the housing subcommittee was for "inclusionary" zoning, meaning that affordable units would be part of the redevelopment plan. In addition, the plan fell short of protecting existing manufacturing, which would result in the displacement of those businesses. Thousands of industrial jobs would be at risk of being lost. Furthermore, open space was inadequate, and waterfront access was piecemeal. Finally, the proposed towers were too tall and bulky, resulting in the loss of sight corridors, and out of character with buildings in the neighborhood (Lander 2004, pp. 6–8). Discussions between the Task Force and various city bureaucrats/specialists ensued, but the clock was ticking and the Community Board had to vote. In line with the Waterfront Rezoning Task Force's recommendation, the Community Board voted to accept the plan with modifications.

The Borough President of Brooklyn, Marty Markowitz, was next to vote. He "opposed an enormous rezoning proposal for Greenpoint and Williamsburg because it did not guarantee enough inexpensive housing, open space or economic stability for people already living in the area" (Cardwell 2005a, p. B1). His vote mimicked the opinion of the Task Force. Markowitz was quoted in the newspaper, saying,

> Many members of the community feel that the administration has developed a proposal for this asset-in-waiting that best serves the constituency of Manhattan . . . This project must serve all Brooklynites, especially the current residents of Williamsburg and Greenpoint" (Cardwell 2005b, p. B1).

Markowitz added to prior criticisms of the administration's plan that rezoning and redevelopment were being done with the affluent and wealthy in mind.

In accordance with a requirement of the New York City Charter, City Planning held a public hearing at a high school in the community in which residents chanted and held banners, "40% GUARANTEE!" while many staged a walk out. Aware of the community's sentiments, the City Planning Commission voted in favor of their plan.

In the meantime, in the New York State Assembly, local representative Vito Lopez sponsored a bill, which was cosponsored by another local representative Joseph Lentol, requiring developers to include a minimum threshold of affordable housing units in order to receive 421A benefits (tax abatements) in the Greenpoint-Williamsburg rezoning site. This bill was justified by the following rationale,

> The original intent of the law establishing the 421A tax abatement as-of-right in Brooklyn was to encourage housing development in an area where market rate development was not occurring and would not occur without the tax abatement. At this time, market rate housing development is clearly occurring and will continue to occur in the defined area without the benefit of the 421A tax abatement. Therefore, the tax abatement is not needed as an incentive to build market rate units (Lopez 2005, p. 2).

On a state level, these local politicians, working on behalf of the community, were attempting to pressure the city administration to revise the redevelopment plan for the waterfront. At this juncture, local elected politicians like Lopez were working on a daily basis with church coalition leaders.

The plan was moved forward to the City Council, where it was first presented to a couple of subcommittees and then to the full Council for a vote. By law, the Council must vote within fifty days. At a meeting of the Zoning and Franchises Subcommittee of the City Council, the council member representing Greenpoint, David Yassky, was quoted,

> I think that this plan needs not just a tuneup or an oil change . . . I think we have to trade this in for a new model and get a rezoning that works for the neighborhood and is not simply designed to allow the builders to build with maximum profitability . . . [If there is no agreement to significant revisions on the part of the Administration] I will be asking you, my colleagues, to join me in rejecting it and starting over" (Cardwell 2005a, p. B3).

This testimony laid the groundwork for negotiations between the City Council, on behalf of the community, and the Bloomberg administration. The Council was prepared to reject the plan if the administration was unwilling to make changes. The night of the City Council's Land Use subcommittee vote, key community leaders sat with Vito Lopez, who talked by telephone with City Council speaker Gifford Miller, Councilmember David Yassky, and Councilmembers Diana Reyna. Through the night and into the early morning these council members communicated between the community (Lopez and leaders) and the Bloomberg administration. These negotiations were tense, and emotions were high on all sides. The administration wanted to complete the rezoning process and was willing to reconsider their approach to open space, parks, and industrial retention. The most stressful part of the negotiations on all sides was over affordable housing. The administration proposed housing vouchers to be used for affordable units.

Lopez vehemently disagreed with this program. He viewed this approach as classist and argued for the inclusion of apartments for ordinary people on the waterfront and in the community. He passionately opposed the use of vouchers for housing that would move ordinary people off the site of rezoning. Lopez could not be dissuaded and held firm to his position. In the end, the administration acquiesced, motivated more by politics than social justice for ordinary people. First, as a State Assembly member, Lopez chairs New York State's housing committee, making and altering legislation dealing with New York City's housing programs. The Bloomberg administration did not need to turn Lopez against them over rezoning the waterfront in his proverbial backyard, his local district. Lopez could become uncooperative on future projects for New York City. Second, Lopez is also leader of the Kings County Democratic Club. His rise to power began as he built the Ridgewood-Bushwick Senior Center, first to provide services, but eventually for a constituency to mobilize to vote as he said (Marwell 2007). Miller, then City Council Speaker, in his plan to run for mayor, supported Lopez in the hope of gaining his and the Democratic Club's endorsement at election time. A revised plan was finally agreed upon by all parties, and the City Council voted to approve the modified plan brokered on behalf of the community and based on the community's terms.

THE FINAL PLAN

The final plan for the waterfront "rezone[s] a 175-block area of Greenpoint and Williamsburg" (Cardwell 2005c, p. 1). It contains fifty-four acres of parks including a publicly run esplanade that spans the entire waterfront. Developers are responsible for constructing their portion of this promenade that will ultimately be turned over to the Parks Department. The plan also specifies an Industrial Business Zone protecting businesses within its confines, and creates a $4 million fund to preserve manufacturing jobs.

Housing development is the most elaborate part of this rezoning package. In order for developers to build to maximum height on the waterfront, which ranges from thirty to forty stories depending on the site (and sites vary depending on their juxtaposition to the low-scale neighborhood), they must include 20 to 25 percent of units affordable to ordinary New Yorkers. Affordability is defined as 80 percent or below of the annual median income of the city for low-income units and 125 percent or below for moderate income units. This would include maximum incomes (for 2005) from $35,150 up to $91,056 depending on family size and the number of bedrooms needed (*Greenpoint-Williamsburg Inclusionary Housing Program* 2005, p. 6). In exchange for affordable units, developers would be eligible for a twenty-five-year tax exemption. Those developers who choose not to include affordable units on their site would have their buildings limited in height and bulk to about twenty-three to thirty-three stories, and would be ineligible for the tax exemption. In the end, Lopez agrees that affordable units could be developed away from the waterfront through new construction or preservation of existing buildings, but they must be located within the neighborhood. These "upland" units would retain tax exemptions. Additional city-owned properties were committed to further increase the total number of affordable units as part of the rezoning plan, such as a closed police precinct and hospital, sludge tank, and the air rights to a bus depot. The estimate is that 3,548 units of affordable housing will be created out of a total of about 10,500 units (Son 2005). Provisions to the final plan include penalties for anyone harassing or displacing tenants because of redevelopment or market forces. A $2 million fund is also being created for tenant advocacy and legal services. This final version is "among the most ambitious such programs in the nation . . . and is the scene of the city's broadest test of inclusionary zoning" (Cardwell 2005c, p. B6). It presently serves as a model for redevelopment. The redefined 421A program, along with inclusionary zoning and density bonuses, are the latest tools used by the Bloomberg administration and the New York City Council to create affordable housing. The community of Greenpoint is moving forward with "contextual rezoning" to prevent the further development of out-of-scale buildings by establishing height limits.

CONCLUSIONS

Ultimately, the "40% GUARANTEE" turned out to be more like 33 percent. This amount is larger, however, than the initial promise made by a major developer to the church coalition. This developer said that he "might" be able to create 5 percent affordable housing with church support for rezoning and city subsidies. The final outcome of rezoning and the redevelopment plan for the waterfront is bittersweet for Greenpoint. On the one hand, the community was involved in the process and made an important contribution. If nothing else, rezoning unburdened the community of the constant threat of toxic polluters locating there. Moreover, the community forced the issues for parkland, open space, public access to the waterfront, and affordable housing. "A Greener New York City" and "Affordable Housing" became strategic areas of the Bloomberg administration, which originated from the rezoning process in Greenpoint.

The community also achieved the greatest amount of affordable housing units ever negotiated in one redevelopment project, and the plan makes future inclusion of them attractive to developers. In addition, this waterfront plan included the working class in the concept of affordability. The focus was not on the currently stigmatized notion of "low income housing" but also housing for those who make this city operate "by the sweat of their brows" and work to preserve it everyday. These are the Greenpointers, the Brooklynites, and the New Yorkers who find themselves in the precarious position of being unable to afford life here. The redevelopment plan gives them some hope of managing, and it also gives priority for affordable units to residents. Finally, the working class community of Greenpoint exercised their power by organizing through the traditional institutions of the Catholic Church and its hierarchy of bishops and the local political club. This amounts to a huge, grassroots constituency with political clout in New York City.

In the years ahead, Greenpoint will no longer be the same place in which many residents grew up and lived. Gentrification and development will continue. The plan for the waterfront development may be stalled by the current economic crisis in the United States, but it may eventually commence making neighborhood change by social class irreversible. The slow, multiyear, decade-long timetable for actually bringing affordable housing units to fruition will be too long and too few for current Greenpoint residents who are struggling to hold on to their apartments and their neighborhood.

Chapter Eight

Conclusions: What It Means for the Future of the City

CAN WORKING CLASS COMMUNITIES BE PRESERVED?

In the summer of 2007, a young firefighter named Daniel accidentally fell to his death from the roof of a building in Williamsburg, fighting what was considered a small fire. As the story unfolded, it was learned that the fire was caused by a smoldering cigarette butt left on the windowsill by a tenant who also used the space as an artist's studio (Gallahue, Weiss, and Alpert 2007). The building was "a former factory converted into apartments and filled with artists" (Gallahue, Weiss, and Alpert 2007, p. 5). The building's certificate of occupancy still listed it as a factory, so technically it was occupied illegally.

Daniel's death reverberated through the community of Greenpoint like a shock wave. Conversations were overheard on the street with nostalgic remarks such as, "I remember that kid from Little League." Photographs of Daniel were placed in the windows of some retail stores on Manhattan Avenue. Daniel had grown up in Greenpoint, the middle son of working class parents who themselves grew up in Greenpoint as the children of working class families. Daniel and his family were very active and involved in the community of Greenpoint. He attended a local Catholic elementary school, played Little League baseball as well as church league basketball (sponsored by the Catholic Youth Organization) for his parish, while his parents volunteered for church and youth activities throughout the neighborhood. They were and remain entrenched in many local, social networks. With their working class values and work ethic, Daniel's parents climbed the proverbial ladder of success, and after many years achieved middle class status through higher education. Both of them are employed as teachers. They are part of the group of residents discussed in a previous chapter who grew up working class and secured middle class status through formal education and unrelenting work. They continue to rent and live in Greenpoint.

The juxtaposed image of Daniel falling to his death from the roof of a building inhabited illegally by artists is a metaphor for the class struggle and eventual destruction that gentrification brings to stable, multigenerational, working class communities. As is indicated throughout this book, social class is a characteristic that segregates neighborhoods as the classes compete for spaces and places, thereby socially dividing residents along class lines. Social class creates differences in human, social, and economic resources that are transformed into social values and lifestyles. The parallel cultures that presently exist in Greenpoint individually composed of the working class and gentrifiers developed because of these very differences. Throughout the chapters are illustrations of different values, beliefs, and choices based on social class. Nonetheless, social class is not exclusively achieved through individual measures. It is inherited, attained, maintained, and sometimes lost through a combination of structural forces, social opportunities, and life's chances. No matter how social class is obtained, it is a driving force, at times more dominant than race and gender and at other times operating in confluence with race, gender, or other social characteristics. For example, in the case of gentry women in Greenpoint, their social class attracts them to the city to live and work. Having been formally educated, the service economy of New York City serves them well, and living in Greenpoint puts them in close proximity to their jobs and other amenities. In addition, their gendered work of mothering combined with their social class situates them to direct their children toward activities perceived as fitting for their social class.

Gentrification and the ways in which social class differences are revealed in a neighborhood reproduces social inequality and maintains the current system of social stratification. Social class is a relative concept and represents levels of a hierarchy suggesting that the higher one is, the more items and thus better quality of life one has. This is often translated into superiority over others. As discussed in earlier chapters, the gentry in Greenpoint create new community organizations instead of joining existing ones, send their children to schools outside the neighborhood in place of utilizing local schools, and prioritize open space and aesthetics over affordable housing and job retention. Such choices convey a belief of relative superiority that is frequently manifested as arrogance. Neighborhood interactions demonstrate that the human, social, and economic capital of gentrifiers differentiates them as superior to their working class neighbors. This leads them to realize, pursue, and achieve what is perceived as "a cut above" for their children relative to working class children. The typical posture of gentrifiers is condescending toward ordinary people. There is a conceitedness conveyed by the gentry;

that as a social class, they view the world with more intelligence and insight and arrive at better conclusions than their working class neighbors. As such, it is not surprising that gentry families operate in a parallel culture to other neighborhood residents.

One may contend that there is a possibility that the gentry do not participate in the neighborhood with working class residents and operate in a parallel culture precisely because they "feel" unliked. If this is the case then one must ask, why would they be unliked? Ordinary, working class people are witnessing the destruction of their community; housing is unaffordable for family and friends, so they are forced to live elsewhere. Homeowners are seeing record increases in real estate taxes due to a spiraling rise of assessed home values due to gentrification. Families and networks of friends living in close proximity to each other are torn apart. Long-term and lifelong neighbors are displaced, being replaced by gentrifiers paying higher prices and driving up the market rate. Local retail establishments, which served as neighborhood landmarks, are forced to close. On some level, ordinary residents connect the changes they witness in their neighborhood to the broader changes of life in the United States. They understand it through experiences of an ever increasing cost of living, unemployment, the changing labor force, and the fact that advanced formal education is no longer directly linked to high-paying work and career. Ordinary people often wonder about where the gentry "get this kind of money"? This question is a reference to gentrifier after gentrifier paying a million dollars for purchasing a house in Greenpoint. These are the same houses that locals were familiar with growing up and saw an increase in price, but homeownership remained within their reach as a stable, working class community. Newer, wealthier residents are viewed with wonder and amazement, but the issue is larger than gentrifiers and gentrification. The handiwork of global, unregulated capitalism has brought about all of the changes that ordinary residents have witnessed in Greenpoint. "There is an elephant in the room that no one is mentioning. That elephant is global capitalism. Global capitalism destroys communities!" (DiFazio 2007). Investments that appear to be local are actually occurring on a global scale by global power brokers who seek new markets and greater profits no matter the human cost.

With economic restructuring in the United States comes gentrification. Gentrification is now a tool of global capitalism in which working class communities are replaced by the affluent and elite. "Mom and pop" retail establishments, which are part of the social fabric of a community, earn a living owning and operating small businesses that were in some cases inherited from their parents, are replaced by large chain stores, such as Starbucks, Rite Aid, and Staples. Housing, both rental and homeownership, becomes out of reach for ordinary people. And the creation of rental housing in particular is replaced by privatized condominiums. ". . . The more recent and still ongoing privatized urban renewal [is] called gentrification . . ." (Gans 2007, p. 232). These changes occur locally within the context of economic restructuring in which the gentry fare better economically in the job market and ordinary people struggle to earn a living wage and avoid catastrophe and to "hang on" to a standard of life with the hope that they will raise their children to have a relatively better life. This is particularly difficult in New York City, but conditions may be still worse for their children.

This is the course of Greenpoint as depicted by this analysis. Greenpoint is experiencing the imposition of global capitalism, a process that can not be completely stopped by the community. The symbols of globalization mentioned above are having an impact on Greenpoint. Residents bid farewell and extend warm wishes to the owners of some of their favorite stores who seemed forever embedded in the neighborhood landscape. These retailers can no longer compete locally with trendy boutiques, organic food and health food stores, thrift shops, "stoop sales," and farmer's markets. These establishments sell goods that are often too expensive for ordinary people. In the view of working class culture, thrift shops and stoop sales were often reserved for poor people no matter how "retro" and "vintage" items may be; from a working class perspective, they remain used or secondhand, a sign of poverty. In contrast, the gentry frequent them and purchase items from them. On a citywide level, megastores like Best Buy, Target, ToysRUs, and online shopping also hurt long-term merchants. As one walks Greenpoint's major commercial strip, Manhattan Avenue, more storefronts with "FOR RENT" signs are seen with speculation regarding the next occupant, or the possibility of no occupancy because of the rising cost of all rents, including commercial space.

On this same walk one observes new construction everywhere. There is a boom of new housing that will not cater to the needs of ordinary residents but hopes to attract more gentry. Ordinary people cannot afford this housing. These are privatized condominium developments, a type of "urban spectacle" (Kern and Wekerle 2008) that stand out of place among the nineteenth and early twentieth century buildings. As Kern and Wekerle point out in their study of Toronto, condominiums, as a new form of built environment, foster social space in which residents turn inward to amenities within the development. They contribute to gentrification and the maintenance of parallel cultures in Greenpoint between the long-term, ordinary residents and newer gentrifiers.

For the neighborhood of Greenpoint, these practices have negative consequences. Greenpoint finds itself divided by social class. As neighborhood issues develop, as with rezoning the waterfront from manufacturing to residential use, which requires community input, many self-interested voices will be heard. For the most part, the working class and immigrant groups with their respective local institutions unite for neighborhood preservation, while the gentry, as a group, present concerns such as aesthetics, recreational spaces, and property values, under the guise of community support. The policies of the Bloomberg administration favor new, privatized development over honoring working class and ethnic neighborhoods. The private sector, often made up of commercial developers, are turned to as investors and builders. The strategy of the Bloomberg administration has been to require the creation of affordable units by private developers in exchange for land use zoning changes that then allow greater height and bulk of new towers and tax abatements. Developers would not be interested in investing and building unless gentrification were proceeding, almost like insurance, to lighten their financial risk. The quandary for ordinary people is that to take an antidevelopment position would mean that no affordable units get built. New developments would, therefore, have buildings with less height and bulk than is possible and also fewer units, but all would be market rate. In areas rezoned, this trade off creates direct conflict between the working class and gentrifiers. These competing interests must somehow be negotiated.

Social segregation by the gentry and the maintenance of their own community within the neighborhood does not create diversity in their community, but rather homogeneity. These actions produce a rather insular group. As a group, their political and social rhetoric is a contradiction given the everyday life they create and experience in Greenpoint. On the one hand their political open-mindedness places them in a position to favor human diversity. Their neighborhood of residence, Greenpoint, is both culturally and economically diverse, but they choose to rebuff it. The actions of the gentry suggest that they remain cautious about social integration with working class and immigrant residents and are unwilling to fully engage in the community with them. Paradoxically, ethnic, working class residents and their everyday lives make up the same working class culture that the gentry initially found attractive. Ordinary residents provide a mixing of race, class, and ethnicity. As the gentry move forward in colonizing Greenpoint, the neighborhood's composition will be primarily white and affluent. Thus, in the final analysis, gentrification also leads to racial and ethnic segregation as well as segregation by social class.

This brings us back to Daniel. Daniel lived and worked to sustain New York City everyday by the proverbial sweat of his brow. Daniel lost his life; the working class has lost, too. The younger children of Greenpoint families have forever lost their working class neighborhood. Daniel's younger brother, who followed in his footsteps as a firefighter, and his friends are doing everything that is socially right. They are following the prescription to acquire the American Dream, but most will not have the ability to buy or even rent in Greenpoint like their parents. The underlying class struggle that is symbolized and underscored by this tragic event begs the questions: Where will ordinary people and the working class be located in the city? Where will they find a place? Will they be directed toward cheaper and poorer areas, which are also diminishing, or will they be supported through urban policy designed to preserve working class communities? The current economic crisis may eventually have an upside for ordinary people. Marx saw crisis as opportunity. The present economic upheaval in the United States, with a record number of housing foreclosures resulting in the bankruptcy of major financial institutions as well as ordinary people, may represent an antithesis to unregulated capitalism. Discussions are already underway regarding "new" ways to regulate banking. Unfortunately, ordinary people have been lured into living above their means by institutions engaged in gluttonous lending practices and are now accused of financial irresponsibility. Moreover, once again, the captains of capitalism will not lose; the federal government will bail them out. However, given this crisis, housing costs may correct and stabilize somewhat, condominiums may remain empty since mortgages will be more difficult to obtain, and the focus on privatized housing may be transformed, with those already built being marketed instead as rentals. These possible outcomes, of course, also presume that ordinary people do not lose their jobs and more in the interim.

To look to global capitalism with resignation as a completely unstoppable force reduces humanity to pawns on a chessboard waiting to be overtaken. In New York City, gentrification, rezoning, and development continue to occur in all five boroughs. The most recent plan is for 125th Street in Harlem, which will transform it from four- and five-story buildings with retail at street level to office towers and market rate condominiums. ". . . The Bloomberg administration has now rezoned more than 6,000 blocks since 2002 . . ." (Williams 2008, p. B3). Harlem's brownstones are already owned by gentry.

The gentry blame developers and capitalists for neighborhoods becoming ever increasingly upscale but fail to recognize their role in the process. This point was illustrated during a live music event at a local bar in which a musician opened her set by criticizing gentrification through a comment about the displacement of artists. Her remarks were met by a reply shouted by a working class patron, "You mean like you've done to us?" As gentry reside in the city while attending school, for short-term fun, or as a long-term living arrangement, they change the very character of working class neighborhoods. The hope is that with each economic crisis comes greater class consciousness for ordinary people. They must continue their activism, their use of traditional institutions as vehicles for social change, their efforts to reach out and build coalitions, and their constant push for greater participatory democracy. As Piven (2006) so aptly affirms in *Challenging Authority: How Ordinary People Change America*,

> My point in this book is not to lay out a blueprint for the future, but to show that all of our past experience argues that the mobilization of collective defiance and the disruption it causes have always been essential to the preservation of democracy (p. 146).

As this study indicates, global capitalism is not always entirely successful in realizing its objective. Local communities can mediate and mitigate structural and global forces on behalf of ordinary people.

Regardless of economic conditions, what seems imperative for a racially, culturally, and economically diverse city is urban policy that is socially just and even-handed and considers everyone equitably. It must be recognized that gentrification and its eventual attendant development is not the solution to a slumping economy, a means to make more money while exploiting others, or a response to a myriad of urban problems.

We need an urban policy that appreciates the contribution of working class citizens to the larger society, as they literally build, repair, and protect, while also creating culturally diverse and economically stable neighborhoods and cities. To choose instead to celebrate massive development by the rich for the young, affluent class and others like them will result in the obliteration of the working class. Urban policy that is socially fair-minded and responsible for all citizens knows that these are deliberate choices to be made and understands the value of preserving working class neighborhoods and communities. It is only then that we will have the opportunity to truly consider the future of the city. The rights of all people as citizens must be a crucial part of the discourse as we plan for neighborhoods and local developments, make policy changes, and simply walk down the street with mutual concern for our shared neighborhood and common humanity no matter our race, creed, or social class.

Bibliography

Abu-Lughod, J. L. *From Urban Village to East Village: The Battle for New York's Lower East Side*. Cambridge, MA: Blackwell, 1994.

Ackelsberg, M. A. "Communities Resistance and Women's Activism: Some Implications for a Democratic Polity." Pp. 297–313 in *Women and the Politics of Empowerment*, edited by A. Bookman and S. Morgen. Philadelphia: Temple University Press, 1988.

Alonso, W. (1980). "The Population Factor and Urban Structure." In *The Prospective City: Economics, Population, Energy and Environmental Developments,* edited by A.P. Solomon. Cambridge: MIT Press, 1980.

Anderson, E. *Streetwise*. Chicago: University of Chicago Press, 1990.

———. *Code of the Street*. New York: W.W. Norton, 1999.

Bahrampour, T. "City Seeking to Rezone Brooklyn Waterfront," *New York Times*, Thursday, June 18, 2003.

Berry, B., and Y. Cohen. "Decentralization of Commerce and Industry: The Restructuring of Metropolitan America." In *The Urbanization of the Suburbs*, edited by L. Mazotti and J. Hadden. Urban Affairs Annual Review, vol. 7. California: Sage, 1973.

Bondi, L. "Gentrification, Work, and Gender Identity." In *Women, Work and Place.* edited by A.L. Kobayashi. New York: Queen's Press, 1994.

Borer, M. I. "The Location of Culture: The Urban Culturalist Perspective." *City & Community* 5, no. 2 (2006): 173–97.

Boyd, M. "Defensive Development: The Role of Racial Conflict in Gentrification." *Urban Affairs Review* 43, no. 6 (2008): 751–76.

Brantlinger, E. *Dividing Classes: How the Middle Class Negotiates and Rationalizes School Advantage*. New York: Routledge Falmer, 2003.

Brooklyn Union Gas Company. "Greenpoint" unpublished pamphlet, sponsored by the Brooklyn Union Gas Company, 1.

Bush, M. E. *Breaking the Code of Good Intentions: Everyday Forms of Whiteness.* Lanham, MD: Rowman & Littlefield Publishers, Inc, 2004.

Cardwell, D. "Brooklyn Rezoning Plan Assailed," *New York Times*, Saturday, January 15, 2005(a).

———. "Council Threatens to Block Plan to Rezone in Brooklyn," *New York Times*, Tuesday, April 5, 2005(b).

———. "City Backs Makeover for Decaying Brooklyn Waterfront," *New York Times*, Tuesday, May 3, 2005(c).

Castells, M. *The City and the Grassroots*. Berkeley: University of California Press, 1983.

Caulfield, J. *City Form and Everyday Life: Toronto's Gentrification and Critical Social Practice*. Toronto: University of Toronto Press, 1994.

Chin, T., and M. Phillips. "Just Play? A Framework for Analyzing Children's Time Use." *Sociological Studies of Children and Youth* 9 (2003): 149–178.

The Church's Response to the Affordable Housing Crisis in Greenpoint/Williamsburg. Thursday, April 22, 2004.

Confessore, N. "Cuomo Moves Toward Lawsuit Over a 50-Year-Old Oil Spill in Greenpoint," *New York Times,* Friday, February 9, 2007.

Cybriwsky, R. "Social Aspects of Neighborhood Change." *Annals of the Association of American Geographers* 68 (1978): 17–33.

DeSena, J. N. *Protecting One's Turf: Social Strategies for Maintaining Urban Neighborhoods*. Lanham, MD: University Press of America, 1990.

———. "Local Gatekeeping Practices and Residential Segregation." *Sociological Inquiry* 64, no. 3 (1994): 307–21.

———. "Low Income Women and Community Power." *Sociological Spectrum* 18, no. 3 (1998): 311–32.

———. *People Power: Grass Roots Politics and Race Relations*. Lanham, MD: University Press of America, 1999.

———. "Gendered Space and Women's Community Work." Pp. 275–97 in *Research in Urban Sociology* Volume 5, edited by R. Hutchison. JAI Press, 2000.

———. *Protecting One's Turf.* Lanham, MD: University Press of America, 2005.

DiFazio, W. *Longshoremen*. Bergin and Garvey Publishers, 1985.

———. Discussion on Gentrification at the Annual Meeting of the American Sociological Association, August 10-14, New York City, 2007.

Duncan, J., and D. Ley. *Place/Culture/Representation*. London: Routledge, 1993.

Duncan, O. D., and B. Duncan. *The Negro Population of Chicago: A Study of Residential Succession*. University of Chicago Press, 1957.

Fava, S. F., and J. N. DeSena. "The Chosen Apple: Young Suburban Migrants." Pp. 305–22 in *The Apple Sliced*, edited by V. Boggs, G. Handel, and S. Fava. Bergin and Garvey Publishers, 1984.

Fitch, R. *The Assassination of New York*. New York: Verso, 1993.

Freeman, L., and F. Braconi. "Gentrification and Displacement: New York City in the 1990s." *Journal of the American Planning Association* 70 (2004): 39–52.

Freeman, L. *There Goes the Hood*. Temple University Press, 2006.

Friedenfels, R. "Gentrification in Large American Cities from 1970–1980." Pp. 63–93 in *Research in Urban Sociology: Gentrification and Urban Change* Volume 2, edited by R. Hutchison. JAI Press, 1992.

Gallahue, P., M. Weiss, and L. I. Alpert. "Eager Hero Took Roof Man's Place," *New York Post*, Saturday, June 23, 2007.
Gans, H. J. *The Urban Villagers*. The Free Press, 1962.
———. "The Sociology of Space: A Use Centered View." *City & Community* 1, no. 4 (2002): 329–40.
———. "A Comment on Borer's 'Cultural Turn'." *City & Community* 6, no. 2 (2007): 157.
———. "But Culturalism Cannot Explain Power: A Reply to Borer." *City & Community* 6, no. 2 (2007): 159–60.
———. "Remembering *The Urban Villagers* and Its Location in Intellectual Time: A Response to Zukin." *City & Community* 6, no. 3 (2007): 231–36.
Gibbs, L. *Love Canal*. Albany: State University of New York Press, 1982.
Gittell, M., and T. Shtob. "Changing Women's Roles in Political Volunteerism and Reform of the City." *Signs: Journal of Women in Culture and Society* 5 (1980): 64–75.
Glazer, N., and D. P. Moynihan. *Beyond the Melting Pot: The Negroes, Puerto Ricans, Jews, Italians, and the Irish of New York City*. Cambridge: MIT Press, 1970.
Goffman, E. *The Presentation of Self in Everyday Life*. Edinburgh: University of Edinburgh Social Sciences Research Centre, 1959.
"Going Greenpoint." *Time Out New York*, May 31–June 6, 2007.
Greenline. "Loft Regulations Urged," March 2001, 1.
———. "Skyrocketing Rents," March 2001, 1.
Greenpoint Gazette. July 8, 1980, 1.
———. December 23, 1980, 1.
Greenpoint-Williamsburg Inclusionary Housing Program. The City of New York, September, 2005.
Greenpoint YMCA. Unpublished Program Catalogue, 2006.
GWYSL Newsletter, November 2005.
Hackworth, J. "Postrecession Gentrification in New York City." *Urban Affairs Review* 37 (2002): 815–43.
Handel, G. "A Children's New York: Boys at Play in Yorkville." In *The Apple Sliced*, edited by V. Boggs, G. Handel, S. Fava. Massachusetts: Bergin and Garvey Publishers, 1984.
Haywoode, T.L. "Working Class Feminism: Creating a Politics of Community, Connection, and Concern." PhD diss., The City University of New York, New York, 1991.
Hemphill, C. *Public Middle Schools: New York's Best*. New York: Soho Press, 1999.
Hofferth, S., and J. F. Sandberg. "How American Children Spend Their Time." *Journal of Marriage and Family* 63 (2001): 295–308.
Holloway, S. L. "Local Childcare Cultures: Moral Geographies of Mothering and the Social Organization of Pre-School Education." *Gender, Place and Culture* 5, no. 1 (1998): 29–53.
Kaplan, T. "Female Consciousness and Collective Action: The Case of Barcelona, 1910–1918." *Signs: Journal of Women in Culture and Society* 7 (1982): 545–66.

Kasinitz, P. "The Gentrification of 'Boerum Hill': Neighborhood Change and Conflict over Definitions." *Qualitative Sociology* 11, no. 3 (1988) 163–82.

Kern, L., and G. Wekerle. "Gendered Spaces of Redevelopment, Gendered Politics of City Building." In *Gender in an Urban World*, edited by J.N. DeSena. The Emerald Publishing Group, 2008.

Krase, J. *Self and Community in the City*. Washington, DC: University Press of America, 1982.

Krauss, C. "Blue Collar Women and Toxic Waste Protests: The Process of Politicization." Pp. 107–17 in *Toxic Struggles*, edited by R. Hofrichter. Philadelphia: New Society Publishers, 1993.

Lander, B. "Rezoning Greenpoint-Williamsburg: What Does It Really Mean for the Community?" Presentation for community leaders, January 12, 2004.

Lareau, A. *Unequal Childhoods*. Temple University Press, 2003.

Laska, S., and D. Spain. *Back to the City: Issues in Neighborhood Renovation*. New York: Pergamon Press, 1980.

Lawson, R., and S. Barton. "Sex Roles in Social Movements: A Case Study of the Tenant Movement in New York City." *Signs: Journal of Women in Culture and Society* 6 (1980): 230–47.

LeGates, R.T., and C. Hartman. "The Anatomy of Displacement in the United States." Pp. 178–203 in *Gentrification of the City*, edited by N. Smith and P. Williams. Allen and Unwin, Inc, 1986.

Levy, P. R., and R. A. Cybriwsky. "The Hidden Dimensions of Culture and Class: Philadelphia." Pp. 138–55 in *Back to the City: Issues in Neighborhood Renovation*, edited by S. B. Laska and D. Spain. New York: Pergamon Press, 1980.

Liebow, E. *Tally's Corner*. Boston: Little, Brown and Company, 1967.

Lofland, L. "The 'Thereness' of Women." In *Another Voice*, edited by Marcia Millman and Rosabeth Moss Kanter. New York: Anchor Books, 1975.

Long, L. H. "The City-Suburb Income Gap." Washington DC: Special Demographic Analyses, U.S. Bureau of the Census, 1980.

Lopata, H.Z. "The Polish American Family." In *Ethnic Families in America*, edited by C. H. Mindel and R. W. Haberstein. New York: Elsevier, 1976.

Lopez, V. "An Act to Amend the Real Property Tax Law in Relation to Certain Real Property Tax Exemptions." Bill Summary. New York State Assembly, Friday, April 15, 2005.

Lutrell, W. "The Edison School Struggle: The Reshaping of Working Class Education and Women's Consciousness." Pp.136–56 in *Women and the Politics of Empowerment*, edited by A. Bookman and S. Morgan. Philadelphia: Temple University Press, 1988.

Marcuse, P. "Abandonment, Gentrification, and Displacement: The Linkages in New York City." Pp.153–57 in *Gentrification of the City*, edited by N. Smith and P. Williams. Allen and Unwin, Inc, 1986.

Markusen, A. (1981). "City Spatial Structure, Women's Household Work, and National Urban Policy." In *Women in the American City*, edited by C. R. Stimpson, E. Dixler, M. J. Nelson, and K. B Yatrakis. Chicago: University of Chicago Press, 1981.

Martin, L. (2008). "Boredom, Drugs, and Schools: Protecting Children in Gentrifying Communities." *City & Community*, 7(4), 331–346.

Marwell, N. P. *Bargaining for Brooklyn: Community Organizations in the Entrepreneurial City*. University of Chicago Press, 2007.

Marx, K., F. Engels, S. Moore, and G.S. Jones. *The Communist Manifesto*. Penguin Classics, 2002.

"Mayor Bloomberg's Chancellor" [Editorial], *New York Times,* July, 30, 2002, 18.

McCourt, K. *Working Class Women and Grass Roots Politics*. Bloomington: Indiana University Press, 1977.

Mead, G. H. *Mind, Self, and Society*. Chicago: University of Chicago Press, 1934.

Mills, C. "Myths and Meanings of Gentrification." Pp. 149–70 in *Place/Culture/Representation*, edited by J. Duncan and D. Ley. London: Routledge, 1993.

Monti, D. J. *The American City: A Social and Cultural History*. Blackwell Publishers, 1999.

Muniz, V. *Resisting Gentrification and Displacement: Voices of Puerto Rican Women of the Barrio*. Garland Publishing, 1998.

Naples, N. A. "'Just What Needed To Be Done': The Political Practice of Women Community Workers in Low Income Neighborhoods." *Gender & Society* 5 (1991): 478–94.

——. "Activist Mothering: Cross Generational Continuity in the Community Work of Women from Low-Income Urban Neighborhoods." *Gender & Society* 6 (1992): 441–63.

——. *Grassroots Warriors*. New York: Routledge Press, 1998.

New York City Department of City Planning. Population: 2000 Census Summary." New York: Author, n.d.

New York City Department of City Planning."Population: 2000 Census Summary," July 30, 2002.

New York City Landmarks Preservation Commission. "Brooklyn Survey: Greenpoint, Proposed Historic District."

New York City Planning Commission. "Greenpoint: Striking a Balance between Industry and Housing." New York, 1974.

Park, R. *The City: Suggestions for the Study of Human Nature in the Urban Environment*. Chicago: University of Chicago Press, 1925.

Piven, F. F. *Challenging Authority: How Ordinary People Change America*. Rowman & Littlefield Publishers, Inc, 2006.

Piven, F.F., and R.A. Cloward. *Poor People's Movements: Why They Succeed, How They Fail*. New York: Vintage Books, 1977.

Reiss, M. *Greenpoint Neighborhood History Guide*. The Brooklyn Historical Society, 2001.

Robinson, T. "Gentrification and Grassroots Resistance in San Francisco's Tenderloin." *Urban Affairs Review* 30, no. 4 (1995): 483–513.

Robson, G., and T. Butler. "Coming to Terms with London: Middle Class Communities in a Global City." *International Journal of Urban and Regional Research* 25, no. 1 (2001): 70–86.

Rose, D. "Rethinking Gentrification: Beyond the Uneven Development of Marxist Urban Theory." *Social Space* 1 (1984): 47.

Ryan, M. "Affordable Housing: The People Come Out in Force." *Greenline* (May 6–31, 2004).

Scott, R. "Inclusionary Zoning: A Proposal for North Brooklyn and New York City." Unpublished report, 2003.

Smith, D. E. *The Everyday World as Problematic: A Feminist Sociology*. Boston: Northeastern University Press, 1987.

Smith, N. *The Urban Frontier: Gentrification and Revanchist City*. New York: Routledge Press, 1996.

Son, H. "Mike Makes Housing Deal," *Daily News*, Tuesday, May 3, 2005.

Spain, D. *How Women Saved the City*. Minneapolis: University of Minnesota Press, 2001.

Steinhauer, J. "Mayor Envisions Housing Revival Unmatched Since the 80's," *New York Times*, December 9, 2002.

Susser, I. *Norman Street*. New York: Oxford University Press, 1982.

———. "Working Class Women, Social Protest, and Changing Ideologies." Pp. 257–71 in *Women and the Politics of Empowerment*, edited by A. Bookman and S. Morgen. Philadelphia: Temple University Press, 1982.

U.S. Bureau of the Census. *Census of Population and Housing: Summary Tape File 3,* 1980: http://factfinder.census.gov, accessed January 30, 2007.

U.S. Bureau of the Census. *Census of Population and Housing: Summary Tape File 3A*, 2000: http://factfinder.census.gov, accessed June 6, 2007.

Wellisz, C. "If You're Thinking of Living in Greenpoint," *New York Times*. December 12, 1982.

Williams, T. "In Park Plan, A New Life for Spaces Long Closed," *New York Times*, Thursday, April 26, 2007.

———. "Council Approves Rezoning of 125th Street, over Loud Protests of Some Spectators," *New York Times*, May 1, 2008.

Wittberg, P. "Perspectives on Gentrification: A Comparative Review of the Literature." Pp. 17–46 in *Research in Urban Sociology: Gentrification and Urban Change*, edited by R. Hutchison. JAI Press, 1992.

Young, A. H., and J. Christos-Rodgers. "Resisting Racially Gendered Space: The Women of the St. Thomas Resident Council, New Orleans." Pp. 95–112 in *Marginal Spaces* edited by M. Smith. New Jersey: Transaction Publishers, 1995.

Zukin, S. *Loft Living*. Johns Hopkins University Press, 1982.

———. "Gentrification: Culture and Capital in the Urban Core." *Annual Review of Sociology* 13 (1987): 129–47.

———. "What's Space Got to Do with It?" *City & Community* 1, no. 4 (2002): 345–48.

Index

www.ingramcontent.com/pod-product-compliance
Ingram Content Group UK Ltd.
Pitfield, Milton Keynes, MK11 3LW, UK
UKHW041625031026
15587UKWH00001B/75

9 780739 123423